"*My New Roots* is beautiful proof that eating with nutrition in mind need not be a compromise. This is an unabashedly enthusiastic riff on the food-as-medicine approach to cooking and eating. Sarah's playful and encouraging voice is infectious; you get the sense that she is waiting on the other side of each recipe to give you a high five."

—HEIDI SWANSON,
author of *Super Natural Every Day*

"Sarah is a veggie-lovin' culinary goddess! Her unique and seasonal plant-based creations will inspire you to fall head over heels in love with vegetables. There are so many beautiful recipes I can't wait to make!"

—ANGELA LIDDON,
author of *The Oh She Glows Cookbook*

"I have been waiting for this book since I first started reading Sarah's blog years ago. She has a gift for writing truly wonderful recipes, vibrant with produce, and has the knowledge to explain why these plant-based foods are good for us. Her sweet spirit shines through every page. So thrilled to have this keeper in my kitchen!"

—SARA FORTE,
author of *The Sprouted Kitchen*

"Sarah always treads the beautiful line between making whole foods practical and also appealing, leading the way in this new real food movement."

—SARAH WILSON,
author of *I Quit Sugar*

"Being healthy and happy is so easy when you're cooking with Sarah. Her gentle approach, love and passion for whole foods, and flair for pairing mind-blowing flavors create fabulous and fresh food that looks stunning and is bursting with personality and life-affirming goodness. With unbelievable tastes and textures, *My New Roots* takes you on an exquisite journey that seduces you with every lift of the fork, leaving you voracious for vegetables."

—TESS MASTERS,
author of *The Blender Girl*

"It's a rare book that delivers inspiration through its every page, yet each one of Sarah's recipes sings with flavor and originality. The entire collection is a seductive introduction to a more wholesome way of eating and an irresistible call to the kitchen."

—CLOTILDE DUSOULIER,
author of *The French Market Cookbook* and *Edible French*

"Sarah's creativity always inspires. With its vibrant recipes, evocative visuals, witty combinations, and approachable ways to live better, this book is a must for anyone interested in optimal, delicious health."

—LAURA WRIGHT,
thefirstmess.com

"*My New Roots* is filled with good ideas for fresh new ways of using plant foods. Sarah Britton shows that truly alive ingredients can result in more interesting and better-tasting recipes and are always worth seeking out."

—DEBORAH MADISON,
author of *Vegetable Literacy* and *The New Vegetarian Cooking for Everyone*

MY NEW ROOTS

My New Roots

INSPIRED PLANT-BASED RECIPES FOR EVERY SEASON

SARAH BRITTON

CLARKSON POTTER/PUBLISHERS
NEW YORK

I dedicate this book to my readers, without
whom this would never have been possible.
Thank you for making my dreams come true.

Published in the United States by Clarkson Potter/Publishers, an
imprint of the Crown Publishing Group, a division of Random House
LLC, a Penguin Random House Company, New York.
www.crownpublishing.com
www.clarksonpotter.com

CLARKSON POTTER is a trademark and POTTER with colophon is
a registered trademark of Random House LLC.

Library of Congress Cataloging-in-Publication Data
Britton, Sarah.
  My new roots / Sarah Britton.
    pages   cm
  Includes index.
  1. Cooking (Natural foods)   I. Title.
  TX741.B68 2015
  641.3'02—dc23   2014018135

ISBN 978-0-8041-8538-7
eBook ISBN 978-0-8041-8539-4

Printed in China
Book and cover design by Marysarah Quinn
Front cover and interior photography by Sarah Britton
Back cover photograph © 2015 by Alan Jensen

10 9 8 7 6 5 4 3 2 1

First Edition

CONTENTS

INTRODUCTION

MY NEW ROOTS BEGAN WITH A TOMATO. It was yellow and shaped like a pear, about the size of a walnut shell. It hung on the vine like a golden teardrop, warming itself in the sun's slanted late afternoon light.

When I put the fruit in my mouth, I immediately noticed the softness and delicacy of its skin. But then I pressed it against the roof of my mouth with my tongue, and it burst into a universe of flavor quite unlike anything I had ever experienced before. It was bright, fresh, grassy, sweet, and overflowing with juice. The tomato tasted of all the things that had made it—the sun, the rain, the soil, the hands that had tended it.

In that moment my life changed. Here I was at twenty-three, a total city slicker, just having graduated from design school and thinking I would be happy behind a computer for the rest of my life. The tomato I picked hung on a vine on an organic farm in Arizona. I was here because it was part of a larger project I had read about during my studies, and I thought it would be a fun experience for a month. Now I was contemplating staying at the farm. Forever.

My whole life I had eaten only processed foods, or fruits and vegetables that had been picked before their ripeness and traveled thousands of miles. I was a sugar addict, overfed and undernourished, never really considering what I ate. I realized with that tomato that food matters, and that we *are* connected to what we eat. That the beauty of the world can be experienced through the taste, smell, and texture of a single fruit. Whole foods became a *revelation*.

The four-week workshop on the organic farm turned into a yearlong, immersive food experience. I ate what we grew, worked the land and my body, gave up processed foods, and the mental fog that I had been living in suddenly lifted. I felt like an entirely new person, *and I was*.

When I returned to Toronto, I had no idea what to do with myself. Something inside me had shifted so strongly toward a life more in tune with the natural world that I knew my direction had to change. I enrolled in the Institute of Holistic Nutrition to deepen my understanding of food and the body and learned that what we eat impacts our health not just on a physical level but on an emotional and spiritual one as well. One day, while I was enthusiastically telling my uninterested boyfriend about all that I was learning, he suggested that I start a blog to share with people who would actually care. Needless to say the relationship didn't last very long, but the blog, *My New Roots*, was born.

Later the same year I ran into a very handsome Dane on a street corner in New York City. Romantic fool that I am, eighteen months later I found myself on a plane, moving to Copenhagen to live with the man who would become my husband. Being in Denmark was wonderful, but professionally I was rather lost. After moving overseas, I discovered that my certification as a holistic nutritionist wasn't recognized, and that it wasn't legal for me to practice. Suddenly I had no direction. Despite the fact that I had no professional cooking experience, my next idea was to apply what I had learned in a restaurant kitchen. I biked around the city handing out résumés to all six vegetarian cafés in hopes of finding a job. The last place I visited was foolish enough to hire me. After destroying many soups with too much cayenne pepper and burning a few lasagnas beyond recognition, I got the hang of cooking and loved it. I developed a new menu each day, using seasonal produce. Because of the ever-changing supply of seasonal fruits and vegetables, I was forced to be creative, think on the fly, and invent new dishes every day. The reaction from diners in the restaurant was overwhelming, and the successes and experiences there were brought to my readers through the blog.

Suddenly requests for cooking classes and lectures started pouring in. Seizing these new opportunities while working full-time in the restaurant and keeping up the blog became nearly impossible. I needed some sort of sign from the heavens on how to handle it all. Unfortunately, this manifested in my husband literally falling out of the sky and breaking both arms in a hang-gliding accident. He was completely dependent on my help twenty-four hours a day—to eat, bathe, dress, or just to make a simple phone call. I had to quit my job to take care of him. Serendipitously, being at home resulted in my having a lot more time to work on the blog and allowed me to focus on projects that I had always wanted to pursue, such as writing for magazines, giving lectures, and teaching cooking classes. As a consequence, *My New Roots* became my full-time job and passion and I haven't looked back since.

Even though *My New Roots* began as a way for me to share what I had learned about wellness and healing, it has become so much more than that. Over the past eight years, through sharing my adventures in the kitchen and my burgeoning obsession with plant-based cuisine, I have inadvertently created a community of readers who are passionate about cooking food that is not only delicious but also very healthy. I found many people hungry for direction and guidance in preparing nutritious food, and discovered that my recipes were actually making significant changes in people's lives. E-mails began flowing in with stories from readers whose families and communities had become more energetic, lost weight, healed from disease, and rediscovered the joy in cooking. *My New Roots* is no longer just my passion project, but a resource that thousands of people turn to every week. Knowing this calls me to the cutting board to create yet another dish to satisfy those who want to take charge of their health and reclaim their kitchens. Their inspiration becomes mine, and the cycle continues. Even though I've never met most of my readers, I can feel us standing side by side at our stovetops, making so much more than dinner.

MY FOOD PHILOSOPHY

I love to eat. A lot. I often joke that my current way of living evolved from needing to find a way to eat a lot and still be healthy. Therefore the diet I follow and encourage others to is not about sacrifice, deprivation, or labels. It is about enjoying delicious food to the fullest extent without counting calories or fat grams. It is about adding healthy, whole-food ingredients to what you are already cooking, taking things slowly, and approaching food with an open mind and a curious belly. I get many e-mails from readers asking for the nutritional breakdown of my recipes, and I can happily tell them that it doesn't matter because *every one* of those calories is good for them. Health is the natural consequence of using whole foods, organic ingredients, and conscious

cooking techniques. What you eat becomes something to celebrate, instead of something to scrutinize. For me that means abandoning diets and embracing this way of eating as a lifestyle, because that is exactly what it is. It is quite simply the most liberating way of eating *and* living.

The recipes in the book are what I call "all-inclusive," meaning they are vegetarian, with options to make vegan versions of the majority, and often gluten-free. I do this so that everyone can use my recipes, even those who have food allergies, sensitivities, or a lifestyle that doesn't include animal products. I use ingredients such as eggs, goat or sheep cheese, and ghee only in certain recipes where I feel it is necessary for flavor or texture, but you can omit them if you like. Overall, I prefer to use the term "plant-based whole foods" to describe my recipes—it makes them approachable even to people who do not label themselves vegetarian or vegan. It is not about what the food is or isn't. The bottom line is, it's delicious and it just so happens to be good for you.

EATING IN THE RHYTHM OF THE SEASONS

A great deal of my cooking inspiration comes from following the seasons. Food is the most intimate connection we have with our Earth, as we literally become the food that we eat. In that sense, eating what is seasonal and local is a priority for me, as this not only helps my body acclimate to the external environment but also contributes to the health of the environment in choosing foods that travel shorter distances. It is not a coincidence that certain foods give us what we need during specific times of the year: high-water-content foods in summer, such as crispy cucumbers and tomatoes cool us down; sweetly rich, starchy, calorie-dense foods like pumpkins and beets to fuel us through the winter. Seasons have a flavor. For me, spring tastes like wild leek pesto: garlicky, green, and youthful. I like to fold it into tendrils of fresh pasta, or slather it on seed-studded toast with avocado and lemon. Autumn tastes like fig and walnut jam: succulent, sun-ripened fruit cooked down slowly with honey, woody thyme, and fragrant lavender into a divine, perfumed love potion.

By taking our cues from nature we align ourselves with the rhythms of the Earth, and consequently our bodies' needs, meanwhile sensually tuning in to the exquisite yet fleeting deliciousness of each cycle.

While I was in school studying holistic nutrition, I was introduced to Traditional Chinese Medicine (TCM), a holistic, integrated system of thinking based on five elements: wood, fire, earth, metal, and water. Each element corresponds to a compass direction, a life stage, a color, a shape, a time of day, specific emotions, internal organs and senses, and a season: spring, early summer, late summer, autumn, and winter.

We are very accustomed to the four-season system in North America and Europe, but if you consider the changes that actually take place during the warmer months, it makes a lot of sense to divide summer into two parts as the Chinese do. This became abundantly clear to me the first time I worked on a farm—as we progressed from early summer to late, the types of produce we were harvesting seemed to be in distinct groups. Early summer has the first really hot weather, bright sun, and long days. Late summer is those last few weeks when it's still warm but the light becomes a deeper golden, the days are noticeably shorter, and you can feel the fall approaching. Since working on many farms and having my own vegetable garden, I now see and feel the benefit of eating with the seasons, and of setting aside extra time for the late summer celebration. In fact, looking back on my life, I can hardly believe I didn't pay attention to it for so long, as it has just become second nature. Although it is customary to divide cookbooks into chapters for each course, I knew when I started to write this book that the seasons would determine the flow. I hope you, too, will fall into the natural rhythm and enjoy connecting with the cycles of the nature all around you—and inside you as well.

As you cook your way through this book, you'll notice that a handful of symbols appear under many of the recipe titles. I hope you'll find them useful as you go about planning your meals.

V the recipe is vegan.

gf the recipe is gluten-free.

◖ the recipe requires planning ahead (such as dough that requires rising) or has a make-ahead element (such as a condiment).

◖ the recipe requires 8 hours or more (to allow for soaking) or is an overnight or long-term project (such as fermentation).

ESSENTIAL TECHNIQUES

The first time I cooked dried beans, I felt like I had discovered the Promised Land. What a triumph! What a revelation! I never imagined that a process that seemed so intimidating could be so easy and practically foolproof, especially for a kitchen novice like myself. I vowed right then and there never to open a can of beans again, and I am proud to say I've kept that promise.

This breakthrough inspired me to see what else I could whip up myself, instead of relying on ready-made and packaged foods from the grocery store. Soon I was cooking whole grains, making ghee, nut milk, and nut butter, and growing my own sprouts. I felt proud and empowered. My food tasted better, cost less, and was healthier than ever.

These are what I call my essential techniques: the very simple and easy-to-learn methods that I use in my kitchen on a daily basis. They form the foundation of much of what I cook at home and many of the recipes in this book. Mastering these easy processes will not only help you cut back on the amount of prepared staples you purchase and save you money but will also give you the confidence you need in the kitchen to tackle anything.

HOW TO COOK DRIED LEGUMES

Dried beans, peas, and lentils make up a large part of the plant-based diet. They are full of satiating fiber, good-quality protein, and health-promoting phytochemicals. Most people shy away from cooking their own because opening a can seems so much easier, but once you get into the habit, you'll see that it takes little time and the benefits are many.

1. Select your legume: Choose organic whenever possible, and look for beans or peas that are relatively uniform in size and color. Do a quick sort and discard any legumes that are cracked or broken, and any stones or debris.

2. Give the legumes a good rinse in a colander under cold running water.

3. Pour the legumes into a pot and cover them with a couple inches of recently boiled water (warm water will also help break down indigestible starches). Add a couple tablespoons of acid, such as lemon juice or apple cider vinegar (2 tablespoons for each 1 cup legumes). Soak for 8 to 12 hours. Drain, rinse again, and return to the (clean) pot.

4. Cover the legumes with plenty of fresh water; it should reach at least 2 inches above the legumes themselves. Add a piece of kombu, 3 to 4 inches long, to the pot. (Kombu, an edible seaweed, has the unique ability to neutralize gas-producing compounds in beans.) Cover, bring to a boil, and skim off any foam that rises to the top. Reduce the heat and simmer until the beans are tender—soft but not mushy. Remove from the heat and add salt: at least 1 tablespoon for each cup of beans, or more to your taste. (Adding salt before this point will prevent the beans from cooking.) Keep the beans covered and let them soak in the salty water for at least 15 minutes and up to 2 hours. Drain, and rinse to remove any excess salt and loose skins.

Although most recipes will tell you not to soak lentils and split peas, I always recommend doing so. It will greatly aid digestion and drastically reduce the cooking time. The chart below indicates the different soaking times.

DRIED LEGUME (1 CUP)	SOAKING TIME	COOKING TIME (AFTER SOAKING)	APPROXIMATE YIELD
ADZUKI BEANS (195G)	NONE, OR OVERNIGHT IF POSSIBLE	30 MINUTES	2½ CUPS / 575G
BLACK BEANS (190G)	OVERNIGHT	45 TO 60 MINUTES	3 CUPS / 515G
BLACK-EYED PEAS (180G)	OVERNIGHT	60 MINUTES	3 CUPS / 600G
CHICKPEAS (185G)	OVERNIGHT	1½ HOURS	3 CUPS / 495G
FAVA BEANS (150G)	OVERNIGHT	45 TO 60 MINUTES	3 CUPS / 510G
GREAT NORTHERN BEANS (185G)	OVERNIGHT	1 TO 1½ HOURS	3 CUPS / 545G
KIDNEY BEANS (200G)	OVERNIGHT	60 MINUTES	3 CUPS / 530G
LENTILS, BLACK (230G)	NONE, OR OVERNIGHT IF POSSIBLE	10 MINUTES	2 CUPS / 400G
LENTILS, DU PUY (210G)	NONE, OR OVERNIGHT IF POSSIBLE	10 TO 15 MINUTES	2½ CUPS / 450G
LENTILS, GREEN/BROWN (200G)	NONE, OR OVERNIGHT IF POSSIBLE	15 TO 20 MINUTES	2½ CUPS / 450G
LENTILS, RED (225G)	NONE, OR OVERNIGHT IF POSSIBLE	10 TO 15 MINUTES	2 CUPS / 400G
LIMA BEANS (150G)	OVERNIGHT	1 TO 1½ HOURS	3 CUPS / 565G
MUNG BEANS (210G)	NONE, OR OVERNIGHT IF POSSIBLE	60 MINUTES	2 CUPS / 200G
NAVY BEANS (185G)	OVERNIGHT	45 TO 60 MINUTES	3 CUPS / 545G
PINTO BEANS (200G)	OVERNIGHT	45 TO 60 MINUTES	3 CUPS / 515G
SPLIT PEAS (210G)	NONE, OR OVERNIGHT IF POSSIBLE	10 TO 25 MINUTES	2 CUPS / 400G
WHOLE PEAS (200G)	OVERNIGHT	30 TO 45 MINUTES	2 CUPS / 400G

HOW TO COOK GRAINS

Whole grains form the foundation of many of my meals. I feel that including a wide variety of unprocessed grains balances my diet and enhances my overall health. It is true that some people cannot tolerate grains, especially gluten-containing ones such as wheat, but that is no reason for everyone to give them up!

UNSOAKED GRAINS

1. Wash the grains well by filling the cooking pot with water, rubbing the grains together, draining, and repeating until the water is clear. Washing the grains removes dirt, excess starch, and in some cases bitter-tasting compounds. Drain well.

2. Add the necessary amount of water and salt (½ teaspoon salt for each cup of grain), and bring the liquid to a boil.

3. Reduce the heat and let the grains simmer, covered, for the designated amount of time, until the grains are tender and the water is absorbed. Do *not* under any circum-stances stir the pot once it is covered! I realize that this is very tempting, but it will interfere with the cooking. To check done-ness, simply insert a fork into the center of the cooking grains and wiggle it back and forth to create a small well so that you can see to the bottom of the pot. If the water is gone, your grains should be ready. Taste for doneness. If the grains are still crunchy, add a little water and cook for a few more minutes.

4. Remove from the heat, and let sit for 5 minutes, covered. Fluff the grains with a fork.

DRIED GRAIN (1 CUP)	WATER FOR COOKING	COOKING TIME (WITHOUT SOAKING)	APPROXIMATE YIELD
AMARANTH (195G)	2 CUPS / 450ML	20 MINUTES	2 CUPS / 500G
BARLEY, HULLED (200G)	3 CUPS / 675ML	60 MINUTES	3½ CUPS / 550G
BUCKWHEAT (200G)	2 CUPS / 450ML	20 MINUTES	4 CUPS / 670G
CORNMEAL/ POLENTA (170G)	4 CUPS / 1 LITER	25 TO 30 MINUTES	2½ CUPS / 400G
COUSCOUS, WHOLE WHEAT (175G)	2 CUPS / 450ML	10 MINUTES (OFF THE HEAT)	3 CUPS / 470G
FREEKEH (185G)	2½ CUPS / 560ML	20 TO 25 MINUTES	3 CUPS / 480G
MILLET (195G)	2½ CUPS / 560ML	20 TO 30 MINUTES	3½ CUPS / 600G
QUINOA (170G)	1¾ CUPS / 400ML	15 TO 20 MINUTES	3 CUPS / 555G
RICE, BLACK (195G)	2 CUPS / 450ML	40 TO 50 MINUTES	3 CUPS / 425G
RICE, BROWN (220G)	2 CUPS / 450ML	30 TO 50 MINUTES	3 CUPS / 425G
RICE, RED (195G)	2 CUPS / 450ML	35 TO 45 MINUTES	3 CUPS / 425G
RICE, WILD (250G)	3 CUPS / 675ML	45 TO 55 MINUTES	3½ CUPS / 570G
SPELT BERRIES (175G)	3½ CUPS / 750ML	25 TO 35 MINUTES	2½ CUPS / 450G
WHEAT BERRIES (180G)	4 CUPS / 1 LITER	45 MINUTES	2½ CUPS / 450G

SOAKED GRAINS

Although it is not necessary to soak grains before cooking them, soaking has its benefits, including removing some of the naturally occurring phytic acid, which inhibits mineral absorption, and breaking down some of the hard-to-digest proteins. Soaking grains also cuts the cooking time down substantially.

1. Wash the grains: Put them in a pot and cover with water. Rub the grains together, drain, and repeat until the water is clear.

2. Cover the grains with warm water (the same amount that you would use to cook the grain), and add 1 tablespoon apple cider vinegar or lemon juice. Stir, and let soak for at least 8 hours and up to 24 hours. Drain and rinse once more.

3. Add one and a half times as much water as the volume of grain (for example, if you originally measured out 1 cup / 170g quinoa, use 1½ cups / 340ml water) and ½ teaspoon of salt for every cup of grain. Bring the liquid to a boil.

4. Reduce the heat and simmer the grains, covered, until the grains are tender and the water is absorbed. Do not stir! If the grains are not fully cooked after the water has been absorbed, add a little more water, ¼ cup at a time, and keep cooking until the grains are tender.

5. Remove the pot from the heat, and let sit for 5 minutes covered. Then fluff with a fork.

HOW TO MAKE GHEE

I was pretty devastated the day I found out that cooking with olive oil wasn't a good idea. If this is news to you, too, well, I completely understand your frustration. But do not despair. I have a trick up my sleeve that will soften your furrowed brow. Introducing *ghee*.

Ghee is one of the best oils for sautéing, roasting, and deep-frying due to its high smoke point (up to 480°F/250°C). As soon as any fat reaches its smoke point, it begins to break down, burn, and create free radicals—those carcinogenic molecules that damage cells and cell membranes and are associated with the development of conditions like atherosclerosis and cancer. Butter burns at a lower temperature because of the presence of casein and lactose. Once those are removed, the smoke point rises. Free radicals no more! The other benefit is that people who are allergic to dairy products, or have casein or lactose intolerance, can often tolerate ghee. Depending on the source of the butter used to make it, ghee can be very high in antioxidants and can help the body absorb vitamins A, D, E, and K and minerals from other foods.

Making ghee is similar to the process of making clarified butter, as both processes remove the proteins (casein) and sugars (lactose), which sink to the bottom of the pot, leaving the pure butterfat on top. Ghee is made by heating unsalted butter for a longer length of time until all the water has boiled off. Ghee is the pure extraction of fat from butter, and it is *insanely* delicious. Think of that warm, caramel-y taste in shortbread or croissants. Ghee is even richer tasting than butter, nutty and deeply satisfying. Whether you're spreading it on toast or drizzling it over veggies, your taste buds will be happy with much less because it is just so darn flavorful.

You can find ghee at most health food stores, but making it yourself at home is about as easy as boiling water. Plus, when you make it yourself, you can choose the quality of the butter. Remember that organic grass-fed cows are the healthiest cows and butter from their milk makes the tastiest ghee.

GHEE

The yield depends greatly on the water content of your butter. Feel free to halve or double this recipe as desired.

1. Set a few layers of cheesecloth or gauze over a sterilized heatproof container, such as a canning jar, and secure them with a rubber band.

2. Heat the butter in a heavy-duty saucepan over low-medium heat until it has melted. Let simmer gently, uncovered, until the foam rises to the top of the melted butter. The butter will make lots of spluttering sounds and perhaps splatter a bit, so be careful.

3. Over the next 20 to 30 minutes (depending on the water content of your butter), watch the butter carefully as three layers develop: a foamy top layer, a liquid butterfat layer, and a milk solids bottom layer. You can remove the foamy top layer with a spoon if you like, which helps to see through to the bottom, but this is optional (it will be strained out in the end anyway).

4. Once the butter stops spluttering and no more foam seems to be rising to the surface, check to see if the bottom layer has turned a golden-brown color. If so, the ghee is ready and must be removed from the heat immediately, or it will burn.

5. Carefully pour the warm liquid butter through the cheesecloth into the container, leaving behind any solids on the bottom of the pan. Let sit at room temperature to cool and solidify before placing an airtight lid on the container. Store the ghee in the fridge for 1 year or in your pantry for 2 to 3 months.

1 pound / 500g organic unsalted butter (do not use salted)

When I gave up dairy milk, I needed to find an alternative. At the time, soy milk was the best replacement available, but after a few years of consuming massive amounts, my hormones got pretty wacky and I had to give it up. I wondered how I would live without any milk at all, until I took a natural foods cooking class where I learned how to make nut and seed milk. Saved!

When you are making nut and seed milk, it is crucial that you soak the foods before. Raw nuts and seeds contain naturally occurring substances that prevent them from sprouting spontaneously and becoming a plant. This is nature's brilliant way of storing genetic material for many years until all the right conditions are in place for the seed to germinate. The problem is that when we consume raw nuts and seeds, we are essentially eating a dormant food, with all of its nutrition locked up inside.

Phytic acid and enzyme inhibitors are two of the substances that we want to remove from nuts and seeds. Phytic acid binds to minerals in the digestive tract, making it impossible for our bodies to absorb them, and consuming phytic acid can even lead to mineral *deficiencies*. Enzyme inhibitors prevent our *own* enzymes from working properly and breaking down the food we are eating. Soaking nuts and seeds in warm salt water helps remove phytic acid and neutralize the enzyme inhibitors, allowing us to absorb and assimilate the vitamins, minerals, and proteins contained within.

Making your own nut or seed milk is incredibly easy. Choose any nut and seed you like, or a combination. Soak, blend, strain, and enjoy.

BASIC NUT OR SEED MILK

MAKES 4 CUPS / 1 LITER

1. Put the nuts or seeds in a glass or ceramic container (or your blender). Cover with the water and add the salt. Soak overnight.

2. Set a nut milk bag over a large bowl or other container (you can also use cheesecloth or even an old T-shirt, but something large enough to contain the pulp and a material you can really squeeze, i.e., not a strainer or sieve).

3. Drain the nuts or seeds and rinse well. (If using almonds, peel them; see Note.) Combine the nuts/seeds and the sweetener in a blender, and blend on high speed for 30 seconds. Strain the mixture through the nut milk bag into the container.

4. Funnel the strained milk into a sealable bottle and store in the refrigerator for 3 to 4 days.

NOTE: If using almonds, it is best to peel them after soaking, as the skin contains some enzyme inhibitors. Simply squeeze the nut and the skin should slide off. If this does not happen easily, your almonds have likely been pasteurized.

1 cup / 140g nuts *or* 1¾ cups / 250g seeds (your nuts/seeds must be raw, organic, and never heat-treated)

1 quart / 1 liter unchlorinated water

Fine sea salt (see below for amounts)

Sweetener of choice and to your taste, such as 2 Medjool dates, 1 to 3 teaspoons raw honey or pure maple syrup, or a couple drops of stevia extract

---

SALT TO 1 CUP NUTS/SEEDS

SOFT NUTS (pecans, walnuts, cashews): 1 teaspoon sea salt
HARD NUTS (almonds, hazelnuts): 1½ teaspoons sea salt
SEEDS (pumpkin, sunflower seeds): 1 tablespoon sea salt

Making your own nut butter has to be one of the most gratifying, life-affirming kitchen pursuits. I liken it to knitting your own scarf or fixing a flat tire on your bike. You could pay someone else to do it, but why bother when you can do a better job yourself and feel pretty darn clever in the process?

This method of making nut butter is easy and will produce a spread with a flavor beyond your wildest dreams. Nothing tastes better than homemade nut butter. *Nothing!* Plus, you'll be paying a fraction of the price of store-bought while avoiding questionable oils, sugar, and preservatives. Yippee!

Making your own nut butter also allows you to be creative: Combine two or more of your favorite toasted nuts and seeds to make delicious nut butter blends, like sesame-cashew, pecan-pumpkin, or almond-hazelnut-sunflower. Add raw cacao for chocolate nut butter too! Cinnamon, ginger, coconut sugar . . . the list goes on as far your imagination can take you.

But, Sarah B, what about those pesky antinutrients?! Good question. You're catching on. Roasting nuts and seeds will most definitely improve their digestibility by removing some of the phytic acid and enzyme inhibitors. (It will not, however, enhance the bioavailability of their vitamin and mineral content.)

NUT BUTTER

MAKES APPROXIMATELY 1 CUP / 250 ML

You can use any kind of nuts for this recipe—almonds, hazelnuts, pecans, and Brazil nuts are all delicious. If you want chunky nut butter, remove a generous scoop of the chopped nuts from the food processor before they turn into a powder, then fold the chopped nuts back into the nut butter before storing.

2 cups / about 280g shelled raw nuts (not roasted or salted)

1. Preheat the oven to 300°F / 180°C.

2. Spread the nuts out in a single layer on a baking sheet and toast until fragrant and slightly darker in color, 20 to 30 minutes. A good way to check if they are ready is to bite one in half and check the color in the center—instead of white or cream colored, it should be golden. Remove from the oven. If using hazelnuts, rub them together to remove their bitter skins. Let cool completely.

3. Transfer the nuts to a food processor and blend on the high setting until finely ground to a powder, 1 to 2 minutes. Stop to scrape down the sides of the container. Continue to process until the oils start to be released and a smooth, creamy, runny paste is formed, 1 to 2 minutes. (Times vary depending on your machine, but it *will* work! Just keep blending; there's no need to add any oil.)

4. Transfer the nut butter to an airtight glass container and store in the refrigerator. It will keep for 1 month.

SEED BUTTER

MAKES APPROXIMATELY 1 CUP / 250 ML

2 cups / about 300g raw seeds (not roasted or salted)

Making seed butter is exactly the same process as making nut butter except that you will want to roast your seeds for a shorter time, 10 to 15 minutes depending on the seed, stirring every few minutes (watch carefully so they do not burn), and add 1 to 3 tablespoons neutral-tasting oil (melted coconut oil or cold-pressed sesame oil works well) once you have processed the seeds into a sandlike texture. Oil will help lubricate the process, but play this by ear; some batches need oil and others do not. It depends on the seed.

Imagine growing a garden in your kitchen. Imagine having fresh raw food, all year round, without needing any outdoor space. Imagine a food that costs pennies to make but has immeasurable health benefits. Imagine boosting your dietary intake of protein, fiber, enzymes, phytonutrients, and pure life force. Stop imagining and start sprouting!

I'm sure you've seen sprouts in their little plastic boxes at the grocery store but passed on them due to the high cost. You also may be wary of the concerns about *E. coli* associated with sprouts. Growing them yourself at home is incredibly inexpensive, and much safer than buying them at the store. I'll teach you how.

First of all, why should we sprout? Sprouting food makes it more digestible because it incites the seed to release its enzymes. Enzymes help the body break down and digest the sprouts, in addition to all other foods we eat with the sprouts. Second, sprouts add delicious fresh flavor and texture to foods. Some sprouts are spicy, some are grassy, tangy, bitter, crunchy, and creamy. Third, growing your own sprouts is easy, fast, and fun.

You can purchase seeds from most grocery stores, health food shops, seed catalogues, and of course online. Dried beans, lentils, and peas are especially easy to find in bulk at natural food shops. It is important to purchase organic seeds, as conventionally grown seeds have often been irradiated prior to storage, and are therefore unable to sprout.

There are several methods for sprouting at home, but I outline the jar method. It's the simplest and most effective way, and you likely have everything you need already!

BASIC SPROUTS

MAKES 4 CUPS / 400G SPROUTS

You will need a glass jar, a piece of fine-mesh window screen or cheesecloth, and a rubber band for this recipe.

1. Measure out the desired amount of seeds, remembering that the volume of the sprouts will be much larger. Sort through the seeds quickly and remove any shriveled, cracked, or discolored ones.

2. Put the seeds in a clean glass jar and cover them with water. Put a screen over the mouth of the jar and secure with a rubber band. Swirl the water around in the jar, rinsing the seeds well, then invert the jar to drain through the screen. Cover the seeds with plenty of fresh filtered water. Let soak for 8 to 12 hours, or overnight.

3. Drain and rinse the seeds through the screen 2 to 3 times. Set the jar at a 45° angle in a bowl or on a dish rack to let it drain. Make sure that any excess water is able to drain out of the jar. Also ensure that the jar will not be sitting in the drained water.

4. Keep the seeds away from the light: Put the jar in a dark area of the kitchen, or cover it with a dish towel. Repeat the rinsing and draining 2 to 3 times a day for 2 to 3 days. The length of sprouting time depends on the sprouts you are growing (see chart, page 28).

5. Once the seeds have sprouted, cover the jar with an airtight lid and store it in the fridge. **NOTES:** The final rinse must precede storage by at least 8 hours so that the sprouts have time to dry out. If the sprouts are wet when you put them in the fridge, they will turn moldy quickly. A word of caution: Large beans, especially kidney beans, need to be lightly cooked or steamed after sprouting to rid them of naturally occurring toxins. They can cause major digestive upset if ingested completely raw. Chickpea, adzuki, mung, and black bean sprouts are okay to eat raw in moderation (maximum 1 cup per day).

3 to 4 tablespoons seeds for sprouting (see chart, page 28)

Filtered water

SPROUT	AMOUNT (FOR A 1 LITER JAR)	SOAK TIME (HOURS)	RINSES DAILY	SPROUTING TIME (DAYS)	ENJOY	SPECIAL NOTES
ADZUKI BEANS	1/3 CUP / 65G	8	3 TO 4	3 TO 6	FRESH OR STEAMED	
ALFALFA SEEDS	2 TABLESPOONS	12	2 TO 3	4 TO 7	FRESH	GREAT STUFFED IN SANDWICHES
ALMONDS	1 CUP / 140G	12	2 TO 3	1 TO 2	FRESH AND/OR DEHYDRATED	WILL NOT DEVELOP A TAIL LIKE OTHER SPROUTS
AMARANTH SEEDS	1 CUP / 300G	8	2 TO 3	2 TO 3	FRESH	
BROCCOLI SEEDS	2 TO 4 TABLESPOONS	8	2 TO 3	3 TO 5	FRESH	SPICY AND DELISH!
BROWN RICE, SHORT-GRAIN	1 CUP / 220G	12 TO 24	2 TO 3	2 TO 4	FRESH OR STEAMED	
BUCKWHEAT	1 CUP / 200G	6	2 TO 3	1 TO 2	FRESH OR STEAMED	VERY SLIMY AFTER SOAKING
CABBAGE SEEDS	2 TO 4 TABLESPOONS	8	2 TO 3	3 TO 5	FRESH	
CASHEWS	1 CUP / 140G	6 TO 8	2 TO 3	1 TO 2	FRESH/AND OR DEHYDRATED	BLEND TO MIMIC DAIRY CREAM
CLOVER SEEDS	2 TABLESPOONS	8 TO 12	2 TO 3	5 TO 6	FRESH	VERY SIMILAR TO ALFALFA IN TASTE AND APPEARANCE
FENUGREEK SEEDS	1/3 CUP / 100G	12	2 TO 3	2 TO 4	FRESH	CURRY FLAVOR
CHICKPEAS	1 CUP / 185G	12 TO 24	2 TO 4	3 TO 4	FRESH	SPROUTED CHICKPEAS MAKE DELICIOUS HUMMUS
KALE SEEDS	1/4 CUP / 75G	6	2 TO 3	4 TO 6	FRESH	
KIDNEY BEANS	3/4 CUP / 200G	8 TO 24	2 TO 3	3 TO 6	STEAMED	EAT IN MODERATION
LENTILS	3/4 CUP / 200G	8	2 TO 3	2 TO 4	FRESH	BLACK, GREEN, DU PUY ARE BEST
MILLET SEEDS	1 CUP / 300G	6 TO 10	2 TO 3	1 TO 3	FRESH OR STEAMED	GOOD ADDITION TO SALADS
MUNG BEANS	1/2 CUP / 210G	8	2 TO 3	2 TO 4	FRESH	THE MOST POPULAR SPROUT IN THE WORLD
MUSTARD SEEDS	3 TABLESPOONS	6	2 TO 3	3 TO 5	FRESH	TASTES LIKE HORSERADISH
OATS, HULLED	1 CUP / 100G	8	2 TO 3	1 TO 2	FRESH OR SLIGHTLY WARMED	
ONION SEEDS	1 TABLESPOON	6	2 TO 3	4 TO 5	FRESH	SPICY
PEAS	1 CUP / 180G	8	2 TO 3	3 TO 4	FRESH	
PINTO BEANS	3/4 CUP / 185G	8 TO 24	2 TO 3	3 TO 6	STEAMED	EAT IN MODERATION
PUMPKIN SEEDS	1 CUP / 300G	8	2 TO 3	1 TO 2	FRESH	
QUINOA	1/2 CUP / 85G	4	3 TO 4	1 TO 4	FRESH OR STEAMED	
RADISH SEEDS	3 TABLESPOONS	6 TO 8	2 TO 3	3 TO 5	FRESH	SPICY
RYE BERRIES	1 CUP / 180G	8 TO 12	2 TO 3	2 TO 3	FRESH	
SESAME SEEDS, UNHULLED	1 CUP / 300G	8	3 TO 4	1 TO 2	FRESH	SOAK WITH 1 1/2 TABLESPOONS SEA SALT
SPELT	1 CUP / 115G	6 TO 8	2 TO 3	2 TO 4	FRESH OR STEAMED	
SUNFLOWER SEEDS, HULLED	1 CUP / 300G	6 TO 8	2 TO 3	2 TO 4	FRESH	SEEDS MUST BE VERY FRESH
TEFF	1 CUP / 200G	4	2 TO 3	1 TO 2	FRESH	
WALNUTS	1 CUP / 140G	6 TO 8	2 TO 3	1 TO 2	FRESH AND/OR DEHYDRATED	BITTER FLAVOR UNLESS DEHYDRATED AFTER SOAKING
WHEAT BERRIES	1 CUP / 180G	10	2 TO 3	2 TO 3	FRESH OR STEAMED	
WILD RICE	1 CUP / 250G	2 TO 3 DAYS	3 TO 4	2 TO 3	FRESH	KEEP IN WATER THE ENTIRE TIME UNTIL RICE IS TENDER

THE HOLY TRINITY OF FLAVOR

There is a famous organic vegetarian restaurant in Copenhagen, Morgenstedet, and I dreamed about working there for a long time until I was persistent enough for them to hire me. My first day on the job, I made a huge batch of soup and asked my very experienced coworker Daniel to taste it. I waited for his response, thinking I had really blown him away with how delicious it was.

He looked at me kind of sideways, then asked me, "What is your acid?"

My *what?*

"In anything you make, you need three things: salt, sugar, and acid. If you don't have all three of those things, your food will always taste like something is missing," he said matter-of-factly and walked back to his cutting board.

I poured a couple glugs of apple cider vinegar into the soup and tasted it. Almost like a miracle, its flavor had been transformed from good to *wow*. It was suddenly rounder, bigger, more complex. I couldn't taste the vinegar, but I could taste how much better the soup was.

So now I call them the Holy Trinity of Flavor: salt, sugar, acid. If you find that your food is on the bland side, go through the checklist to see if you've included all three, and if not, add a dash of whatever you're missing, tasting as you go. It's a simple trick that has really improved the flavor of my meals, and kept my blog readers coming to back to my recipes without even knowing it!

SALT: sea salt, Himalayan rock salt, soy sauce, tamari, miso

SUGAR: raw honey, pure maple syrup, barley malt, brown rice syrup, coconut sugar, dates, fruit juice, applesauce

ACID: citrus juice (lemon, lime, grapefruit), vinegar (apple cider vinegar is the healthiest choice)

NEXT-LEVEL TRICKS

Another important trick I learned while working in professional kitchens is that you can easily take your dish to the next level simply by finishing it off with one, two, or all three of the following: citrus zest, fresh herbs, and lightly toasted nuts or seeds.

Even if all you have is a humble pot of steamed brown rice, if you fold in some lemon zest, parsley, and toasted almonds, suddenly you have a beguilingly aromatic, delicious, and special meal. Or take that same pot of rice, add lime zest, cilantro, and lightly toasted pumpkin seeds, and you have a completely different dish.

SPRING

MORNINGS

STRAWBERRY COCONUT MILKSHAKE

CARROT RHUBARB MUFFINS

FREEKEH PANCAKES WITH WILTED SWISS CHARD
    AND POACHED EGGS

STRAWBERRY CHIA JAM

DARK CHOCOLATE CHERRY OVERNIGHT OATS

SMALL MEASURES

THE LIFE-CHANGING LOAF OF BREAD WITH OLIVES AND CARAWAY

SPRING CABBAGE WRAPS WITH COUSCOUS, ZA'ATAR,
    AND SPICY TAHINI DRESSING

PICK-ME-UP PICKLED TURNIPS

SHAVED TURNIP AND RADISH SALAD WITH POPPYSEED DRESSING

SAVORY SPRING HAND PIES

DANDELION GREENS WITH GHEE-POACHED RADISHES AND
    SMOKED SALT

MAINS

OYSTER MUSHROOM BISQUE

QUINOA RISOTTO WITH GRILLED SCAPES AND ARUGULA

BLACK LENTIL SALAD WITH TZATZIKI, AVOCADO, AND PEA SHOOTS

SPROUTED WILD RICE WITH PISTACHIOS AND SPRING VEGETABLES

SOCCA WITH GRILLED WHITE AND GREEN ASPARAGUS,
    DILL, AND FETA

SWEETS

MOON MACAROONS

APRICOT RHUBARB CLAFOUTIS

STRAWBERRY CHAMOMILE NO-CHURN FROZEN YOGURT

SUNFLOWER SESAME SEED BRITTLE

STRAWBERRY COCONUT MILKSHAKE

SERVES 1

This milkshake is truly decadent and luscious beyond belief. When strawberries are in season, their flavor is so remarkable—and what better way to enjoy them than blended with creamy coconut and floral bee pollen?

Combine the strawberries, banana, coconut milk, lemon zest, and bee pollen in a blender. Add the ice cubes and blend on high speed until smooth and creamy. Garnish with sliced strawberries and a sprinkling of bee pollen.

1 cup / 250g strawberries, plus more for serving

1 frozen banana

1 cup / 250ml coconut milk

Grated zest of ½ organic lemon

1 to 3 teaspoons bee pollen (depending on what you're used to eating), plus more for serving

2 ice cubes

CARROT RHUBARB MUFFINS

MAKES 12 MUFFINS gf

We all know the classic strawberry-rhubarb combination, but this spring I discovered how amazing rhubarb tastes when combined with carrots! With tart rhubarb, rich walnuts, and warming spices, these muffins are almost like a healthy mini carrot cake. Because they are baked with oats instead of flour, they are easy to make gluten-free, and since the applesauce acts as a binder instead of eggs, they are also vegan. Serve these muffins with Strawberry Chia Jam (page 38).

1. Measure out 1½ cups / 150g of the rolled oats and put them in a food processor. Pulse until you have a coarse flour. Put the flour in a large bowl, and add the remaining 1 cup / 100g rolled oats and the coconut sugar, cinnamon, ginger, cardamom, sea salt, baking powder, and baking soda. Stir to combine.

2. Pulse the carrots in the food processor until they are roughly minced. Put the carrots in a medium bowl. Pulse the walnuts a couple of times in the food processor until roughly chopped, and then add them to the carrots. Slice the rhubarb into thin disks and add to the carrots.

3. Preheat the oven to 350°F / 180°C. Lightly grease a muffin tin with coconut oil (or line it with muffin liners).

4. Add the maple syrup and applesauce to the flour mixture, and mix just to combine. Then fold in the carrots, rhubarb, and walnuts.

5. Fill the muffin cups with dollops of the batter; sprinkle with a few rolled oats if desired. Bake in the oven for 25 to 35 minutes, until the muffins are golden and a toothpick inserted in the center comes out clean. Remove from the oven and let cool for 5 to 10 minutes before removing from the tin. Enjoy warm.

2½ cups / 250g gluten-free rolled oats, plus extra for sprinkling if desired

½ cup / 60g coconut sugar

2 teaspoons ground cinnamon

2 teaspoons ground ginger

1 teaspoon ground cardamom

½ teaspoon fine sea salt

1 teaspoon baking powder

½ teaspoon baking soda

4 to 6 spring carrots (about ⅓ pound / 200g), unpeeled, roughly chopped

¾ cup / 105g raw walnuts (optional)

2 thin stalks rhubarb

Knob of coconut oil, for greasing the tin (or use muffin liners)

¼ cup / 60ml pure maple syrup

1 cup / 250g unsweetened applesauce

FIBER Ideally, one should aim for at least 35 grams of fiber a day, and with a healthy whole-foods diet, this is an easy goal to reach.

FREEKEH PANCAKES WITH WILTED SWISS CHARD AND POACHED EGGS

SERVES 4

Perhaps it's because I don't eat meat anymore that I am so attracted to the taste of smoke, but whatever the case, I have a total crush on anything with a fire-kissed flavor. I first discovered freekeh, an ancient grain, at my local Middle Eastern grocery store, and I fell in love with its deep, rich, smoky taste. Freekeh is very similar to cracked wheat or bulgur, with one interesting difference: the grain is made from young green wheat that goes through a roasting process during production, resulting in its signature smoky flavor. If you are looking for a hearty breakfast with plenty of protein, fiber, and slow-burning carbohydrates, these freekeh pancakes are for you.

½ cup / 92g freekeh (will make a little more than 1 cup / 185g cooked freekeh)

Fine sea salt

¼ cup / 30 g whole spelt flour

5 organic eggs: 1 beaten, 4 for poaching

2 scallions, sliced

2 garlic cloves, minced

½ fresh chile, minced (Serrano is a good choice)

½ teaspoon sea salt

Knob of ghee or coconut oil

1 bunch (1 pound / 450g) Swiss chard (8 to 12 leaves), stems removed

Freshly squeezed juice of ½ lemon

Freshly ground black pepper

1. Rinse the freekeh well, drain it, and then put it in a small pot. Add double the amount of water and a few pinches of salt. Bring to a boil, reduce the heat, and simmer, covered, until the water is absorbed and the grains are tender, about 20 minutes.

2. In a large bowl, combine the cooked freekeh with the spelt flour, beaten egg, scallions, half of the garlic, chile, and ½ teaspoon sea salt, stirring until it forms a thick, wet dough that will easily hold together (if it's too wet, add a little more flour; if it's too dry, add a touch of water). Divide the mixture roughly into four portions (approximately ⅓ cup / 75ml per pancake); roll each portion into a ball with your hands and flatten it into a thick patty.

3. Preheat a large skillet or griddle over medium-high heat, and coat it with a little ghee. Reduce the heat and transfer the pancakes to the skillet. Cook until golden on one side, about 5 minutes. Then flip them over and cook for another 5 minutes, until the pancakes are cooked through yet tender. Transfer the cooked pancakes to a plate and cover with a towel until ready to serve.

4. Roll up the chard leaves and slice them into thin ribbons. To cook the chard, heat another knob of ghee in the skillet, add the remaining minced garlic, and cook over medium heat for about 1 minute, until fragrant. Add the chard and cook, stirring constantly until just wilted, about 2 to 3 minutes. Remove the pan from the heat, and sprinkle the lemon juice over the chard.

5. Bring a small saucepan of water to a simmer to poach the eggs. Crack the eggs, one at a time, into a small bowl, and then slip them into the barely simmering water (it helps to stir the water into a whirlpool first, then drop the egg into the center). Cook for 3 to 4 minutes, until the egg whites are just set, and then use a slotted spoon to transfer the eggs to a clean tea towel or paper towel; let them drain until ready to serve (this helps absorb any excess water). If necessary to reheat, put the eggs into the simmering water again for 60 seconds.

6. To assemble, place a pancake on each plate; top each pancake with chard ribbons and a poached egg. Season generously with salt and pepper. Enjoy immediately.

STRAWBERRY CHIA JAM

MAKES ABOUT 2 CUPS / 650G

This jam is based on real fruit, natural sweeteners, and chia seeds—the miracle food that turns liquid into thick jelly, just what jam should be. You won't believe how delicious this totally raw homemade jam is, and how much easier it is to make than the classic cooked version. It whips up in about five minutes and is delicious on top of everything from oats, muffins, and toast to ice cream. If you don't have any of those things on hand, just eat it with a spoon!

1 pound / 500g ripe strawberries

1 tablespoon pure maple syrup
or raw honey

1 tablespoon freshly squeezed
lemon juice

½ vanilla bean, split lengthwise,
seeds scraped out and
reserved

Pinch of fine sea salt

3 tablespoons chia seeds

1. Wash and cut the tops off the strawberries. Put the berries in a food processor, add the maple syrup, lemon juice, vanilla bean seeds, and salt, and blend on the highest setting until smooth.

2. With the food processor running, slowly pour in the chia seeds and process until fully incorporated, 5 to 10 seconds.

3. Scrape the jam into a glass jar with a tight-fitting lid, and store it in the refrigerator until gelled, 15 to 20 minutes. You can keep the leftovers in the fridge for up to 1 week.

CHIA SEEDS Chia seeds are one of my favorite superfoods because they are packed with antioxidants, fiber, complete protein (ideal for vegetarians/vegans), omega-3 and omega-6 fatty acids, calcium, phosphorus, magnesium, manganese, copper, iron, molybdenum, niacin, and zinc. Their best party trick, however, is their ability to absorb nine times their volume in water, providing energy, prolonged hydration, and retention of electrolytes, which is perfect for runners and other athletes. If there is one food to add to your diet, chia seeds are a top contender.

DARK CHOCOLATE CHERRY OVERNIGHT OATS

SERVES 1   V gf ☽

Although it takes some planning ahead, this breakfast is a very special treat. Take a few minutes before bed to assemble the ingredients, pop them in a bowl or jar, and let sit in the fridge overnight. The next morning, your meal is ready to rock; just toss in some fresh fruit and raw chocolate. This is fast food without waiting in the take-out line! If cherries aren't in season, simply substitute any fruit you can find—berries in summer; pears, figs, and apples in autumn; persimmons and pomegranate in winter; and so on. (Dried fruit works as well.)

1. Fold the oats, milk, lemon juice, and chia seeds together in a jar or bowl, cover, and refrigerate overnight.

2. In the morning, remove the muesli from the fridge and fold in the cacao powder, nibs, and maple syrup. Top with the cherries. Add more yogurt or milk if desired. You can also let the muesli stand at room temperature for 10 minutes to warm up slightly. For a pretty presentation, layer the oat and chia mixture with the sliced cherries in a glass jar or bowl.

²/₃ cup / 65g gluten-free rolled oats or any other rolled (gluten-free) whole grain

1 cup / 250ml nut milk of your choice (I like Brazil nut, almond, or hemp), plus more for serving, or 1 cup / 225ml water or 1 cup / 245g yogurt

½ teaspoon freshly squeezed lemon juice (omit if using yogurt to soak grains)

2 tablespoons chia seeds

1½ tablespoons raw cacao powder

2 teaspoons cacao nibs

1 tablespoon pure maple syrup

Sliced fresh cherries

THE LIFE-CHANGING LOAF OF BREAD WITH OLIVES AND CARAWAY

MAKES 1 LOAF (V) (gf) (☾)

There is no way I could write a cookbook and not include the famous recipe that launched *My New Roots* into the blog stratosphere. The life-changing loaf of bread continues to circle the globe, convincing skeptics everywhere that healthy food can also taste delicious. To change things up a tad, I added a couple of my favorite things: caraway seeds and black olives. These little flourishes really make the bread special and even tastier. Keep in mind that the LCLOB (as it is now affectionately known the world over) is a base recipe that you can adapt with just a few additions. If you've never made this bread before, be prepared to fall in love. It makes the most delicious toast, too!

1. In a flexible silicone loaf pan (or a parchment-lined loaf pan) combine the sunflower and flax seeds, hazelnuts, oats, chia seeds, psyllium seed husks, sea salt, and caraway seeds, stirring well.

2. Whisk the maple syrup, oil, and 1½ cups / 340ml water together in a measuring cup. Add this mixture plus the chopped olives to the dry ingredients, and mix until everything is completely soaked and the dough becomes very thick (if the dough is too thick to stir, add 1 or 2 teaspoons of water until it is manageable). Smooth out the top with the back of a spoon. Let sit out on the counter covered for at least 3 hours, or overnight.

3. Preheat the oven to 350°F / 180°C.

4. Bake the loaf on the middle rack of the oven for 20 minutes. Remove the bread from the loaf pan, turn it upside down directly onto the oven rack, and bake for another 30 to 40 minutes. (The bread is done when it sounds hollow when tapped.) Let the bread cool completely before slicing; to slice it easily, use a very sharp, smooth knife instead of a serrated bread knife.

5. Store the bread in a tightly sealed container in the refrigerator for up to 5 days. (It freezes well, too, so slice before freezing for quick and easy toast!)

PSYLLIUM SEED HUSKS This bread does not contain any flour, so the binding agent used is psyllium. Psyllium seed husks are one of nature's most absorbent fibers, able to suck up over ten times their weight in water. For this reason, psyllium helps to reduce cholesterol levels, aid digestion, and augment weight loss. Psyllium has no flavor whatsoever, so you can rest assured that the bread will taste of all the other ingredients.

1 cup / 140g sunflower seeds

½ cup / 90g flax seeds

½ cup / 70g hazelnuts or almonds

1½ cups / 150g gluten-free rolled oats

2 tablespoons chia seeds

4 tablespoons / 32g psyllium seed husks (3 tablespoons / 24g if using psyllium husk powder)

1 teaspoon fine sea salt

1 tablespoon caraway seeds

1 tablespoon pure maple syrup (for sugar-free diets, substitute a pinch of stevia)

3 tablespoons coconut oil or ghee, melted

½ cup / 100g Kalamata olives, pitted and chopped

SPRING CABBAGE WRAPS WITH COUSCOUS, ZA'ATAR, AND SPICY TAHINI DRESSING

SERVES 4

I have a pretty major crush on Lebanese food. There is something about its use of fresh ingredients, lemon, herbs, good olive oil, and copious amounts of tahini that sings to my heart. My inspiration for this meal came from those flavors, but I change up the fillings for these wraps according to the season. This time of year I use my absolute favorite cabbage, an early spring variety that is one of the first to appear in the garden and at the market. Its purple hue looks incredibly appetizing with the green herbs and pea shoots. Its leaves are tender yet crisp, a terrific contrast to the delicate couscous. Of course, the tahini sauce is the star here. Keep the jar of it nearby when you're eating—you'll surely be pouring it on every bite. As a final flourish, sprinkle the magical za'atar topping over the entire meal for a true flavor explosion! These wraps are exceptionally good with the Pick-Me-Up Pickled Turnips (page 45).

1. Put the couscous and salt in a large bowl, and stir to combine. Add the boiling water, stir quickly, and then cover the bowl with a plate or a piece of plastic wrap. Let it sit for 10 minutes. Remove the cover and fluff the couscous with a fork (if the couscous is still slightly crunchy, replace the cover and let it sit for another couple of minutes).

2. Fold in the onion, parsley, olive oil, lemon zest, and olives. Season with salt.

3. Arrange the cabbage leaves on a platter and spoon an eighth of the couscous onto each one. Top with a handful of the beans and some pea shoots. Drizzle with the tahini sauce and olive oil, and sprinkle generously with za'atar and some cracked black pepper. Serve.

COUSCOUS Contrary to popular belief, couscous is not a grain, but rather a very finely crushed form of durum wheat semolina, the same kind used to make pasta. Because the grain has not been ground, it is less processed than pasta and offers more fiber and nutrients, especially in the whole wheat variety—the only type I purchase. I don't eat couscous very often, but it certainly comes in handy once in a while when I need to whip up a meal in a hurry. It cooks in only 10 minutes! If you would like a gluten-free alternative in this recipe, replace the couscous with millet or quinoa.

1 cup / 175g whole wheat couscous

1 teaspoon fine sea salt

1 cup / 225ml boiling water

1 small red onion, sliced

1/2 cup / 10g chopped fresh parsley

1 tablespoon olive oil, plus more for garnish

Grated zest of 1 organic lemon

1/2 cup / 100g whole Kalamata olives

8 whole cabbage leaves (2 per person)

1 cup / 145g cooked butter beans (or any bean you like)

Handful of fresh pea shoots

Spicy tahini dressing (page 44)

Za'atar (page 44)

Freshly cracked black pepper

SPICY TAHINI DRESSING

MAKES ABOUT 1 CUP / 225ML

⅓ cup / 80ml tahini

1 large garlic clove, minced

1½ tablespoons freshly squeezed
   lemon juice

1 tablespoon cold-pressed
   olive oil

¼ teaspoon crushed red pepper
   flakes or cayenne pepper

Pinch of fine sea salt

1 teaspoon raw honey or pure
   maple syrup

Combine the tahini, garlic, lemon juice, olive oil, red pepper flakes, sea salt, and honey in a blender and blend on high speed until completely smooth. (Add water to thin as necessary.) Store in an airtight glass container in the fridge for up to 1 week.

ZA'ATAR

MAKES ½ CUP / 65G

¼ cup / 36g sesame seeds,
   lightly toasted

¼ cup / 50g ground sumac

2 tablespoons dried thyme
   leaves

1 tablespoon dried oregano
   leaves

Combine the sesame seeds, sumac, thyme, and oregano in a bowl, and stir well. Transfer the spice mix to a glass jar and store in a cool, dark place for up to 3 months.

PICK-ME-UP PICKLED TURNIPS

MAKES 1 QUART / 1 LITER

The first time I ate falafel at a Lebanese restaurant, it came with tabbouleh, tahini sauce, fresh tomato slices, and some disturbingly neon-pink sticks of unknown origin that I left alone. Years later, a little braver and whole lot more adventurous, I tried one of those twigs, and I couldn't believe what I'd been missing—pickled turnips, hallelujah! So gorgeously acidic, crispy, and of course a perfect complement to the meal. Then I learned that the unnaturally bright pink does not come from wacky food coloring, but from beets—traditionally added to the pickling jar for an appetizing blush.

Turnips are not the most glamorous or sexy veggie, but here they are transformed into something very special. These are delicious as a side with just about anything: try them on a sandwich, on top of a salad, or in an Abundance Bowl (one of the most popular recipes on my blog). They are the ultimate pick-me-up, and you'll wonder how you ever dismissed these little guys in the first place!

1. Slice the turnips and beets into batons about the size of large French fries.

2. In a large measuring cup, combine the vinegar, maple syrup, and sea salt with 2 cups / 450ml water. Stir to combine and dissolve the salt.

3. Put a few slices of garlic in a 1-quart/1-liter jar, and add the dill sprigs. Toss a handful of turnip batons into the jar, followed by a couple of beet batons and then a few more slices of garlic. Continue layering the turnips, beets, and garlic until you have filled the jar.

4. Pour the pickling liquid over the vegetables. Cover the jar with a tight-fitting lid and keep at room temperature for a week before enjoying. Then store the remaining pickled turnips in the refrigerator for up to 6 weeks.

2 pounds / 1kg turnips, peeled

1 small beet, peeled

¾ cup / 170ml apple cider vinegar

2 tablespoons pure maple syrup

2 tablespoons fine sea salt

2 large garlic cloves, sliced

2 sprigs fresh dill

TURNIPS Caught a cold this spring? Add turnips to your diet! Turnips help reduce mucus in the body, ease lung congestion, and relieve sore throats. They contain good amounts of vitamin C as well, which helps boost the immune system.

SHAVED TURNIP AND RADISH SALAD WITH POPPYSEED DRESSING

SERVES 4

This salad is a surprising and totally raw way to enjoy spring produce. If you've never eaten turnips raw before, you will love their slightly peppery, earthy flavor, especially when combined with the radishes and raw asparagus. If you can find very small or baby asparagus, definitely use them. Spring turnips usually are small and have not yet matured enough to have their purple ring. The entire bulb should be completely white; otherwise they may be tough and bland. This is a rather loose recipe—the real key is making everything taste yummy and look beautiful, so don't worry too much about exact amounts. Just go by taste and aesthetics!

1. Whisk the olive oil, vinegar, lemon zest, mustard, shallot, poppy seeds, honey, and a pinch of salt together in a small bowl.

2. Using a mandoline, slice the turnips and radishes into thin translucent rounds. Put them in a large bowl and add the watercress. If the asparagus are large, slice them in half and add them to the bowl. Pour the dressing over and fold gently to combine.

3. Season with more salt if needed, arrange on plates, and sprinkle with the chives before serving.

RADISHES Radishes are a fabulous food for anyone looking to cleanse and detoxify. They are incredibly effective at breaking up phlegm in the body, especially that resulting from overconsumption of heavy animal products. Radishes contain a lot of water as well, so they are filling but very low in calories, making them ideal for people trying to control their weight. In Chinese medicine, radishes are used to promote digestion, break down mucus, soothe headaches, and heal laryngitis. It is said that regular consumption will help prevent viral infections such as the common cold and influenza.

¼ cup / 60ml cold-pressed olive oil

2 tablespoons apple cider vinegar

Grated zest of 1 organic lemon

1 teaspoon Dijon mustard

½ shallot, diced

1 tablespoon poppy seeds

1 teaspoon raw honey or pure maple syrup

Fine sea salt

2 spring turnips, peeled, tops removed

4 medium radishes, tops removed

1 small bunch watercress

1 bunch asparagus, as young as possible

3 tablespoons minced fresh chives

SAVORY SPRING HAND PIES

MAKES 6 PIES

Looking for a lunch you can take with you on the go? Enter hand pies! Super-tasty and convenient, these little guys are a wonderful make-ahead meal that is about as close to fast food as you can get without the post-snacking regrets. I combine the freshest seasonal produce, including ramps, to make a savory filling that really satisfies. Add more protein with some lentils or beans, if you like. You can use the dough recipe and create a seasonal hand pie for every month this year!

If you cannot find ramps, use the tops of spring onions instead. To make a more tender dough, use half whole spelt and half light spelt.

DOUGH

2 cups / 240g whole spelt flour

½ teaspoon fine sea salt

⅓ cup / 80ml coconut oil or ghee, melted

FILLING

Knob of ghee or coconut oil

2 cups / 60g ramps, chopped (or use 1 bunch spring onions, green parts only)

Fine sea salt

2 garlic cloves, minced

1 cup / 150g shelled peas (fresh or frozen)

¼ cup / 30g capers

Grated zest of 1 organic lemon

⅓ cup / 80g crumbled goat or sheep feta

1 tablespoon caraway seeds

Freshly ground black pepper

1 large egg, beaten with 2 tablespoons water (optional)

Hot sauce for serving, if desired

1. Make the dough: Sift the flour and salt together into a large mixing bowl. Pour in the oil and blend it in with a fork. Mix in a couple tablespoons of water; then add 1 tablespoon at a time, up to ½ cup / 112ml total, until the dough is no longer crumbly. Knead the dough just until it comes together. Do not overwork. Cover the dough with a damp towel and allow it to rest at room temperature for about 1 hour. (You can also wrap and refrigerate the dough overnight.)

2. Preheat the oven to 400°F / 200°C.

3. Make the filling: Heat the ghee in a skillet over medium heat. Add the ramps and a few pinches of salt. Cook until wilted and slightly golden, 7 to 10 minutes. Add the garlic and cook for 1 minute more. Remove from the heat and stir in the peas, capers, lemon zest, feta, and caraway seeds. Season with salt and pepper.

4. Divide the dough into 6 balls. Using a rolling pin, roll out each ball into a 7-inch / 18cm round, as evenly as possible. Put about a sixth of the filling on one side of a dough round and fold the other half over to cover the filling. Press a fork around the edges to seal them. Continue with the remaining dough and filling. Brush the dough lightly with the beaten egg, if desired.

5. Put the hand pies on a parchment-lined baking sheet and bake for 20 to 25 minutes, or until lightly golden. Serve with your favorite hot sauce on the side.

RAMPS Ramps, also known as wild leeks, are not only delicious but loaded with powerful nutrients called flavonoids, my favorite being quercetin. Quercetin is especially effective against seasonal allergies, which is appropriate because so many people suffer from allergy symptoms this time of the year.

DANDELION GREENS WITH GHEE-POACHED RADISHES AND SMOKED SALT

SERVES 2 TO 3

The first time I made butter-poached radishes, I had low expectations, considering how much I loved the crispy, piquant qualities of raw radishes. Not only was this one of the most foolproof processes I've ever tried, it turned those humble radishes into an entirely different vegetable! The once assertive-tasting root became tender and mellow, even a little sweet. (I use ghee to poach these, but you could use butter in a pinch.) I placed these pale-pink beauties on a bed of dandelion leaves because the spiciness of the greens is an amazing complement to the smooth radish flavor. If you cannot find dandelion, arugula would be lovely, too.

1. Slice the radishes in half lengthwise.

2. Melt the ghee in a large skillet over medium heat. Add the garlic and sauté for 1 minute. Then add the radishes, cut side down, and the pinch of salt, and sauté for about 10 minutes, until they are slightly translucent and tender, but not mushy.

3. Drizzle the vinegar over the radishes and toss quickly to incorporate. Remove from the heat and drizzle the honey over the top; toss to coat.

4. To serve, make a bed of dandelion greens on each plate, arrange a portion of the radish halves on top, and pour the pan drippings over the top to dress the salad. Season with smoked sea salt, and enjoy.

1 bunch (½ pound / 250g) radishes, tops removed

2 tablespoons ghee (butter will also work)

2 garlic cloves, minced

Pinch of fine sea salt

2 teaspoons apple cider vinegar

2 teaspoons raw honey or pure maple syrup

1 bunch dandelion greens (about 3 cups)

Smoked sea salt

DANDELION Step away from the lawn mower—did you know that you had a veritable superfood growing in your backyard? I'm talking about dandelion, one of the most nutritious and flavorful greens in the world! Dandelion greens help fight cancer, boost immunity, slow down the aging process, and build bones, teeth, and blood, while protecting the heart against atherosclerosis. They are super-high in beta-carotene, chlorophyll, calcium, iron, and magnesium. If you are going to eat the ones from your lawn, try to harvest them just before they flower, as the flavor becomes too bitter after that. Remember to harvest dandelion greens from an area that has not been treated with fertilizer, pesticides, or any other chemicals.

OYSTER MUSHROOM BISQUE

SERVES 3 TO 4

In early spring, when the weather is still deciding what to do with itself, I bury myself in bowls of soup to get through the last chilly days. This one, a deeply rich, creamy bisque, is a favorite because it is like getting a hug from the inside. Mushrooms are one of the few plant-based foods that offer umami—the elusive fifth taste—due to their abundance of glutamate. Because they are so satisfying, mushrooms often stand in for meat in vegetarian dishes, but one taste of this soup and you will agree that there is absolutely nothing missing. Bisque is often made with dairy, but my version uses blended beans to achieve a luxurious creaminess that mimics heavy cream but is virtually fat-free. In addition, beans deliver healthy vegetarian protein and a serious dose of filling fiber.

Scant ½ pound / 225g oyster mushrooms

1 tablespoon coconut oil or ghee

3 medium onions, chopped

2 large leeks

Fine sea salt

1 teaspoon fresh or dried thyme leaves, plus sprigs for garnish, if desired

4 garlic cloves, minced

Freshly squeezed juice of ½ lemon

1 quart / 1 liter vegetable broth

2 cups / 350g cooked white beans (navy, butter, cannellini, Great Northern)

Freshly ground black pepper

2 tablespoons cold-pressed olive oil

1. Clean the mushrooms by removing any dirt or natural debris with a damp cloth (do not submerge them in water). Chop the mushrooms that are large, leaving the smaller ones intact.

2. Heat the coconut oil in a large pot and add the onions, leeks, a good pinch of sea salt, and the thyme. Cook for 5 minutes over medium heat, until the onions and leeks are soft. Add the garlic to the pot and stir.

3. Sprinkle the lemon juice into the pot and stir to loosen any browned bits. Stir in the mushrooms and cook on medium heat for about 5 minutes until the mushrooms are soft.

4. Meanwhile, combine the vegetable broth and beans in a blender, and blend on high speed until creamy.

5. When the mushrooms are cooked, remove a few from the pot for garnish. Add the broth and bean mixture to the pot, stir well, and simmer for 5 minutes.

6. Ladle the soup into the blender and blend on high speed until completely smooth. Add water or more broth to thin if necessary.

7. Season the soup with plenty of freshly ground black pepper, and with sea salt if necessary. Ladle the soup into bowls, and garnish with the reserved cooked mushrooms, a drizzle of olive oil, and some fresh thyme sprigs. Serve hot.

QUINOA RISOTTO WITH GRILLED SCAPES AND ARUGULA

SERVES 2 TO 3 gf

The carb-worshiper in me loves risotto, but the health nut in me always dreams of something better. It was quite a revelation, then, to discover one could make risotto out of other grains besides white rice. Hallelujah! The first time I cooked up risotto with quinoa was actually kind of a mistake, as I'd added too much stock to the pot but soon realized what I had on my happy little hands: a brothy bowl of delicious bliss.

In this recipe I've added gorgeous grilled garlic scapes and peppery arugula to boost the flavor and lean into the green. Scapes are the flowering tops of hard-neck garlic plants, with a flavor similar to asparagus but with a distinctive garlicky essence. If you cannot find scapes, use spring onions instead.

1. Melt half of the ghee (1 knob) in a large saucepan over medium heat. Add the shallots and sauté until soft and translucent, about 4 minutes. Add the garlic and quinoa, stir to coat, and cook for about 1 minute.

2. Pour in the hot broth and bring to a boil. Reduce the heat and simmer, covered, until the quinoa is tender but still slightly raw, 12 to 14 minutes. Fold in the cheese and cook until the quinoa is al dente and the risotto is still brothy. Remove from the heat and fold in the arugula, which will wilt slightly. Season with salt and pepper.

3. Heat a grill or a cast-iron skillet to medium-high heat.

4. Rub the scapes with the remaining ghee and put them on the hot surface. Grill, turning them once during cooking, until they are tender and slightly charred, 7 to 10 minutes.

5. To assemble, spoon the quinoa onto plates; top with the scapes and more grated cheese if desired. Drizzle with olive oil and sprinkle with plenty of cracked black pepper. Serve hot.

2 knobs of ghee or coconut oil

3 shallots, minced

2 garlic cloves, minced

1 cup / 170g quinoa, well rinsed

2½ cups / 560ml vegetable broth, heated

2½ ounces / 75g grated Pecorino Romano cheese, plus more for garnish if desired

3 cups / 75g arugula

Fine sea salt and freshly cracked black pepper

About 12 garlic scapes, tough ends trimmed

Cold-pressed olive oil

SCAPES Garlic scapes boast many of the same super health-promoting properties that garlic does. We're talking a good dose of manganese to keep your bones strong and healthy and protect cells from free-radical damage, vitamin B_6 to support your nervous system, vitamin C to boost your immune system and improve iron absorption, and selenium to reduce joint inflammation.

BLACK LENTIL SALAD WITH TZATZIKI, AVOCADO, AND PEA SHOOTS

SERVES 3 TO 4

Isn't it funny how the things we love to eat at restaurants are often put in the category "too difficult to make at home"? This was definitely the case with tzatziki. Then the first time I actually endeavored to make it, I was struck by how incredibly easy it was and just how much better it tasted fresh from my own kitchen. This dish is a simple spring salad bowl with fresh flavors and satisfying textures.

1 cup / 230g black lentils, soaked if possible

Fine sea salt

1 cup / 180g green olives, pitted and roughly chopped

1 shallot, minced

¼ cup / 5g chopped fresh parsley

2 tablespoons cold-pressed olive oil, plus extra for garnish if desired

Grated zest and juice of 1 organic lemon

½ teaspoon raw honey or pure maple syrup

2 ripe avocados, pitted and sliced

Handful of fresh pea shoots

Tzatziki (page 57)

1. In a medium saucepan, bring the lentils and 2 cups / 450ml of water to a boil. Cover and simmer on low heat until the lentils are tender but not mushy, 15 to 25 minutes (depending on soak time, if any). Halfway through cooking, add a few pinches of salt. When the lentils are tender, drain off any excess water.

2. Put the lentils in a large bowl and add the olives, shallot, parsley, olive oil, lemon zest and juice, honey, and salt to taste. Fold to combine.

3. To serve, put a few spoonfuls of lentil salad on each plate. Top each serving with slices of avocado, some pea shoots, and a generous dollop of tzatziki. Drizzle with extra olive oil if desired.

FOLATE Lentils are one of the yummiest sources of folate (also known as folic acid)—just 1 cup / 200g of cooked lentils provides you with almost 90% of your daily recommended allowance! And why is folate so important? You've probably heard about this vital vitamin in regards to pregnancy, as it is critical in the prevention of birth defects. Folate also functions to support red blood cell production and help prevent anemia, allows nerves to function properly, helps prevent osteoporosis-related bone fractures, and helps prevent dementias, including Alzheimer's disease.

TZATZIKI

1. Put the yogurt in a large bowl.

2. Grate the cucumber into a separate bowl and squeeze out as much liquid as possible. Add the squeezed cucumber to the yogurt.

3. Add the olive oil, garlic, dill, and lemon juice, and fold to combine; season with salt and pepper. Chill in the refrigerator for at least 1 hour before serving, to allow the flavors to combine. Store any leftovers, covered, in the fridge for up to 2 days.

1 cup / 245g thick yogurt (Greek-style works well, or strained goat or sheep yogurt)

½ English cucumber, unpeeled

2 tablespoons cold-pressed olive oil

1 to 2 garlic cloves, minced

2 tablespoons minced fresh dill

Freshly squeezed juice of ½ lemon

Fine sea salt and freshly ground black pepper

SPROUTED WILD RICE WITH PISTACHIOS AND SPRING VEGETABLES

SERVES 4

Sprouting wild rice is a simple and delicious way to enjoy this amazing food completely raw. The process of sprouting wild rice is called "blooming" because the seeds actually unfold, very much like little petals, revealing the pale, tender insides. It's a really fun thing to watch, however slowly, and it's groovy to eat something you've seen transform over a few days.

This salad combines fresh springtime tastes and textures, all sauced up with a delicious dressing featuring bright lemon and spicy mustard. The herbs add the final layer of flavor, making this a salad that truly tastes alive! Because the rice is sprouted, it is very sweet, requiring salt in the salad—make sure to season it well to suit your own taste.

1 cup / 200g wild rice (makes 1½ cups sprouted rice)

2 tablespoons cold-pressed olive oil

2 tablespoons strong mustard

Grated zest of 1 organic lemon

2 tablespoons freshly squeezed lemon juice

1 teaspoon pure maple syrup

Fine sea salt

2 cups / 300g shelled green peas

1 cup / 165g cooked chickpeas

4 spring carrots, julienned

⅓ cup / 7g chopped fresh chives

⅓ cup / 7g chopped fresh dill

⅓ cup / 40g raw pistachios, roughly chopped

1. Rinse the rice well, put it in a glass jar or bowl, and cover with fresh, pure water. Let soak on the countertop overnight.

2. In the morning, drain and rinse the rice; then cover it again with fresh water and put the jar in the fridge. Drain and rinse the rice at least twice per day for 2 to 3 days, until it has "bloomed"—some or all of the grains will have split open, and it should be tender enough to eat. Drain and rinse the sprouted rice and put it in a large bowl.

3. Whisk the olive oil, mustard, lemon zest and juice, and maple syrup together in a small bowl, adding a few pinches of sea salt. Pour half of the dressing over the rice and fold to coat. Stir the peas, chickpeas, carrots, and herbs into the rice.

4. In a dry skillet over medium heat, toast the pistachios until golden and fragrant, about 5 minutes (be careful not to burn them!). Add the toasted nuts to the salad. Pour the remaining dressing over and fold to combine. Serve.

WILD RICE Wild rice is the wildly nutritious seed of an aquatic grass that contains high levels of protein, fiber, iron, and calcium. It is also gluten-free and extremely high in folic acid.

SOCCA WITH GRILLED WHITE AND GREEN ASPARAGUS, DILL, AND FETA

SERVES 4

The first time I made socca, a traditional Provençal flatbread (called *farinata* in Italian), I was really excited. For someone who is pretty obsessed with warm, starchy baked goods, these high-protein, gluten-free crepes were a revelation! I like to make a double batch, cook them all at once, and store the extras in the freezer for a future meal when I'm in a rush. They make wonderful stand-ins for tortilla wraps and pizza bases. This version of socca is covered in sweet caramelized onions and smoky grilled asparagus, but feel free to use any seasonal veggies. It makes a really lovely lunch served with a side salad.

1. Slice the onions into thin rounds. Heat the ghee in a large skillet, add the onions and a few pinches of salt, and stir to coat. Cook over medium-low heat, stirring occasionally. When the pan becomes too dry, add a little of the balsamic vinegar. Cook until the onions are golden and caramelized, 20 to 25 minutes, or longer if necessary. Transfer the cooked onions to a bowl.

2. Snap off the hard bottoms of the asparagus stalks. Peel the white asparagus if the stalks are thicker than your finger (it tends to be tough on the outside with the peels left on). Rub the asparagus spears with a little melted ghee.

3. Preheat a grill or grill pan until hot.

4. Put the asparagus on the grill and cook, turning them over once, until tender and slightly charred, 5 to 10 minutes (depending on the thickness of the spears).

5. To assemble, put a socca on each plate, cover with a quarter of the caramelized onions, a few asparagus spears, a generous sprinkling of dill, and a few spoonfuls of feta. Season with salt and pepper. Drizzle with olive oil if desired. Serve warm.

4 medium onions (1 pound / 500g)

A few knobs of ghee or coconut oil

Fine sea salt

2 teaspoons balsamic vinegar

1 bunch (generous ½ pound / 300g) green asparagus

1 bunch (¾ pound / 370g) white asparagus (use green asparagus if you cannot find white)

Socca (page 62)

1 bunch fresh dill, chopped

2½ ounces / 75g goat or sheep feta (optional)

Freshly cracked black pepper

Cold-pressed olive oil for garnish, if desired

CHICKPEA FLOUR Chickpea flour is a tasty alternative to other gluten-free flours. It has an amazing, creamy consistency and a rich flavor. It is higher in protein than wheat flour and is a good source of folate, iron, and magnesium.

SOCCA

MAKES 4 CREPES

1 cup / 90g chickpea flour

¾ teaspoon fine sea salt

½ teaspoon freshly cracked
   black pepper

1¼ cups / 280ml warm water

3 tablespoons ghee or coconut
   oil, melted, plus more for
   cooking the crepes

1. In a large bowl, sift the chickpea flour, salt, and pepper together. Whisk in the warm water and melted ghee. Let sit, covered, at room temperature for at least 30 minutes. (I recommend making this before you leave the house in the morning, to enjoy the socca for dinner that same day.)

2. In a large skillet, melt a knob of ghee over high heat. When the ghee is very hot, pour about a quarter of the batter in and tilt the pan so that it coats the bottom evenly as one large crepe. Cook for 5 to 8 minutes, until there are bubbles forming on the surface and the batter turns from shiny to opaque (you know that the pancake has set at this point). Flip the socca and cook for a couple of minutes, just long enough for it to brown (alternatively, you can set the skillet a few inches below your broiler to cook the second side). Remove the socca from the pan and cover it with a clean tea towel, or keep it warm in the oven, until ready to serve. Repeat with the remaining batter. (You can freeze finished crepes: once they are completely cooled, put them into a sealable plastic bag, remove as much air from the bag as possible, and seal the bag. To reheat, put on a baking sheet in a warm oven.)

MOON MACAROONS

MAKES 28 MOONS (NATURALLY)

I love making nut milk, so I am always trying to invent ways to use up the leftover pulp. These moon macaroons have turned out to be an excuse to make the nut milk in the first place! They are so satisfying, rich, and delicious—the perfect little treat when I just need a bite of something sweet. I call them "moon macaroons" because I like to dip them in the chocolate following the moon phase calendar, just for kicks.

This recipe teaches you how to make coconut butter and raw dipping chocolate. Both taste dangerously delicious yet remain virtuous because they are made with whole-food goodness. You can use them in many other applications (try spreading the coconut butter on toast, or throw a dollop into a smoothie; use the raw chocolate to dip fruit), so let your creative sweet tooth run wild!

1. Make the macaroons: In a large mixing bowl, combine the coconut, coconut butter, nut pulp, lucuma, vanilla seeds, maple syrup, and salt. Take a small amount of the mixture in your hands and squeeze firmly. If the mixture holds together, it is the perfect consistency—if not, add a little more maple syrup and coconut butter, 1 teaspoon at a time, until the mix holds together. Roll into 1-inch / 2.5cm balls and put on a piece of parchment paper. Put in the freezer (this will make dipping in chocolate easier).

2. Make the raw dipping chocolate: Melt the coconut oil, cacao butter, and maple syrup together in a double boiler (or a tempered glass bowl set over simmering water) over low-medium heat and stir to combine. Sift in the cacao powder and salt. Whisk until completely smooth.

3. Remove the double boiler from the stove and while the chocolate is still liquid, dip the frozen macaroons, either completely (remove with a fork to let excess chocolate drip off) or just halfway. Put on a piece of parchment paper and let dry.

MACAROONS

2 tablespoons unsweetened shredded coconut

2 tablespoons coconut butter (page 64), or more if needed

½ cup / 64g nut pulp from making 1 batch nut milk (see page 23)

2 tablespoons lucuma powder

1 vanilla bean, split lengthwise, seeds scraped out and reserved

2 tablespoons pure maple syrup, or more if needed

¼ teaspoon fine sea salt

RAW DIPPING CHOCOLATE

2 tablespoons coconut oil

1 tablespoon cacao butter

2 tablespoons pure maple syrup or raw honey

¼ cup / 30g raw cacao powder

Pinch of fine sea salt (optional)

(RECIPE CONTINUES)

NOTE When making raw chocolate, it is essential that all equipment be completely dry or the chocolate will seize up and you'll have to start over.

4. Let the chocolate set completely before storing the macaroons in a tightly sealed container in the freezer, where they will keep for 1 month. Stored in the fridge, they will keep for 3 to 4 days.

COCONUT Some people are still afraid of coconut's fat content. Coconut oil does contain saturated fat, but luckily for us, the fat comes in the form of medium-chain triglycerides, or MCTs. This type of fat differs from the types we normally consume from both plant and animal sources, which are long-chain triglycerides, or LCTs. Without getting too technical, MCTs are easily digested, absorbed, and utilized in the body because their molecules are smaller than those in LCTs. This means that, unlike other fats, they require less energy and fewer enzymes to break them down for digestion. They are an excellent choice of fat for active people and athletes, as MCTs can be digested immediately to produce energy and stimulate metabolism. They are also ideal for those who suffer from digestive disorders and are often given in hospitals to provide nourishment for critically ill people who have trouble digesting fat.

COCONUT BUTTER

MAKES ABOUT ³/₄ CUP / 120G ⓥ ⑨

2 cups / 185g unsweetened shredded coconut

In a food processor or high-speed blender, blend the coconut until it becomes a liquid, scraping down the sides of the machine often (this can take anywhere from 2 to 20 minutes). Pour the contents into a glass jar, seal it tightly, and store at room temperature for up to 3 months.

APRICOT RHUBARB CLAFOUTIS

SERVES 8 (gf)

Cla. Foo. Tee. Sounds like a fancy, intimidating, impossible-to-make-at-home dessert, doesn't it? I had the same feeling once, but now this is one of the most frequently made desserts in my house, especially when I have guests to impress. Not only because it's incredibly delicious, but because it is so darn easy to make. This version includes two spring fruits that pair very well together—sweet apricots and sour rhubarb—but you can make clafoutis any time of the year with whatever happens to be in season. Cherries are the most traditional, and berries are delicious, too. Don't let the fact that my adaptation is dairy- and gluten-free put you off; this dessert is rich, velvety, and lusciously springtime!

1. Preheat the oven to 350°F / 180°C.

2. Spread the almonds on a baking sheet, and bake until fragrant, about 15 minutes. Remove from the oven and let cool. Leave the oven on.

3. While the almonds are roasting, slice the apricots into quarters and the rhubarb into very thin slices. Rub just a little coconut oil on the bottom of a 9-inch / 23cm tart pan or other shallow ovenproof baking dish. Scatter the fruit in the pan.

4. In a food processor, pulse the cooled, toasted almonds until very finely chopped, so that they resemble sand—but don't go too far or you'll have almond butter! Add the brown rice flour, coconut sugar, vanilla seeds, eggs, egg yolks, coconut milk, and salt, and blend until smooth.

5. Pour the batter over the fruit and bake for 45 minutes, until the top is golden brown. Serve warm.

¾ cup / 105g whole raw almonds

8 medium fresh apricots

2 slim stalks rhubarb

Coconut oil, for greasing the pan

2 tablespoons brown rice flour

¾ cup / 90g coconut sugar

1 vanilla bean, split lengthwise, seeds scraped out and reserved, or 1 teaspoon vanilla extract

2 large eggs

2 large egg yolks

1 cup / 250ml full-fat coconut milk

Pinch of fine sea salt

EGGS Although I try to make my recipes vegan, there are times when nothing but an egg will do. If you are going to eat eggs, find a good source: getting to know a farmer is your best bet, but because that isn't always realistic, try to purchase pasture-raised, organic eggs that have been produced locally. Eggs are an excellent source of high-quality animal protein that provides a complete range of amino acids. Eggs also contain a variety of minerals, such as selenium and iodine, that support normal thyroid function and are difficult to find in other sources.

STRAWBERRIES These berries contain a vast array of antioxidant and anti-inflammatory nutrients, as well as essential vitamins and minerals. Strawberries are the best-known fruit source of vitamin C, and one of the best fruit sources of manganese. They help regulate blood sugar, support cardiovascular health, and aid in the prevention of certain cancers.

STRAWBERRY CHAMOMILE NO-CHURN FROZEN YOGURT

MAKES 1 QUART / 1 LITER

Cooking with tea has become a new passion of mine. I had never really thought about it until I tried a delicious cookie made with Earl Grey tea. That little biscuit lit a spark in me, as I saw the potential in using different teas as spices in both sweet and savory dishes. The idea for this tea-infused yogurt came from snacking on freshly picked strawberries and iced chamomile tea one steamy summer afternoon. It was a delightful combination, and I thought a frozen treat with these two flavors would be just divine. Oh my, was I ever right! There is something about the perfumed sweetness of strawberry with the mellow floral warmth of the chamomile that just works. It's a unique and unexpected twist on a classic summer favorite. (Although this recipe doesn't require an ice cream machine, feel free to use it if you have one.)

1. Roughly chop about one-quarter of the strawberries.

2. Combine the remaining whole strawberries, honey, chamomile flowers, vanilla seeds, yogurt, and lemon zest and juice in a blender and process until completely smooth, making sure that there aren't any unblended bits of dried chamomile in the mix. Pour the contents of the blender into a 9-inch / 23cm square metal pan and fold in the chopped strawberries. (If you have an ice cream maker, use it now, following the manufacturer's instructions.)

3. Freeze the yogurt for 45 to 60 minutes. Then remove the pan from the freezer and use a fork or a sturdy whisk to whip the yogurt until creamy (this will help discourage ice crystals from forming). Return the yogurt to the freezer and repeat the whisking every 30 minutes for up to 2 hours, making sure the yogurt is as smooth as possible every time before returning it to the freezer.

4. Cover the container with plastic wrap and store it in the freezer. Remove from the freezer 10 or 15 minutes before serving. (The yogurt can be kept for up to 2 weeks.)

14 ounces / 400g strawberries

½ cup / 113ml raw honey or pure maple syrup

¼ cup / 5g organic dried chamomile flowers (or enough tea bags to equal ¼ cup flowers)

1 vanilla bean, split lengthwise, seeds scraped out and reserved

3 cups / 735g full-fat plain yogurt (goat, sheep, or cow)

Grated zest of 1 organic lemon

1 tablespoon freshly squeezed lemon juice

SUNFLOWER SESAME SEED BRITTLE

SERVES 6 TO 8

When I was little, my mother and I used to make peanut brittle for special occasions. I remember melting the sugar in the pot and watching the temperature on the candy thermometer climb as the caramel bubbled away. I still love the idea of this treat, so years later I've figured out a way of making it much healthier, using sunflower and sesame seeds in place of peanuts, and brown rice syrup instead of processed sugar. It's still salty-sweet with an extreme crunch, but much less allergenic and easier on your blood sugar levels.

1. Preheat the oven to 325°F / 170°C. Line a rimmed baking sheet with parchment paper.

2. Combine the sunflower seeds, coconut, sesame seeds, cranberries, salt, and cinnamon in a large mixing bowl and stir well.

3. In a small saucepan, melt the coconut oil over low heat. Add the syrup and whisk until uniform. Pour the liquid over the dry ingredients and fold quickly to incorporate it before the mixture becomes too sticky. Spoon the mixture onto the prepared baking sheet and smooth out the top with the back of an oil-greased spatula.

4. Bake for 15 to 20 minutes, until golden brown. Let cool completely on the baking sheet.

5. Using the edges of the parchment as handles, lift the cooled brittle off the baking sheet, and put it on a work surface. Crack the brittle into pieces, and store them in a sealed container at room temperature for up to 2 weeks. (If you used barley malt syrup, keep the finished product in the freezer if you want it to be crisp, or at room temperature for a chewy brittle.)

1¼ cups / 175g sunflower seeds

½ cup / 45g unsweetened shredded coconut

¼ cup / 35g sesame seeds

½ cup / 75g dried cranberries or raisins, roughly chopped

1 teaspoon fine sea salt

1 teaspoon ground cinnamon

2 tablespoons coconut oil

½ cup / 120ml brown rice syrup

SUNFLOWER SEEDS Sunflower seeds are an excellent source of vitamin E, the body's primary fat-soluble antioxidant, benefiting the body's cardiovascular system. Sunflower seeds also contain good amounts of magnesium, a natural relaxant that helps calm nerves, muscles, and blood vessels.

EARLY
SUMMER

MORNINGS

ROOIBOS GINGER SUN TEA

MULTIGRAIN CARROT CAKE PORRIDGE WITH PECAN CRUNCH

TEMPEH MUSHROOM BREAKFAST BOWL

FULLY LOADED BREAKFAST BARS

SMALL MEASURES

SORREL HUMMUS

LABNEH WITH ROSE PETALS, SESAME, AND HONEY

CARROT TOP AND GARLIC SCAPE PESTO

GRILLED ZUCCHINI AND GREEN ONIONS WITH BABY SPINACH
AND HAZELNUTS

THE REAL DEAL GINGER ALE

MAINS

CARAMELIZED ONION, OLIVE, AND KALE CALZONES

FULL-BLOOM ARUGULA SALAD WITH MILLET, RED CURRANTS,
AND NASTURTIUMS

CARAMELIZED FENNEL ON HERBED POLENTA

THAI-STYLE COCONUT SOUP WITH ZUCCHINI NOODLES

FAVA BEAN, SWEET PEA, AND TARRAGON SOUP

SWEETS

MINT CHIP ICE CREAM SANDWICHES

THE RAW BLONDIE

RASPBERRY MACADAMIA THUMBPRINT COOKIES

PIÑA COLADA PASSION FRUIT POPSICLES

ROOIBOS GINGER SUN TEA

MAKES 1 QUART / 1 LITER

I have a serious aversion to turning on the stove in the heat of summer, so my solution for brewing tea is to use the awesome power of the sun. Sun tea has been around for a very long time, but it seems that the only people who know about this simple process are the original hippies. I think it's time for this really groovy idea to make a comeback, so here goes!

You can make sun tea using any tea you like, or even fresh herbs—lemon balm, mint, and verbena are particularly refreshing. You can also use sun tea to make naturally brewed soda (see page 90).

1. Pour 4 cups / 1 liter unchlorinated water into a sterilized glass container.

2. Wrap the ginger and loose tea in a piece of cheesecloth and tie with a string. Drop the cheesecloth bag into the water and put the container in direct sunlight; leave it for 3 to 5 hours. (If you are using tea bags, wrap the ginger in cheesecloth and add the tea bags separately.)

3. Remove the cheesecloth bag and put the container in the fridge; the tea will keep for 3 to 4 days. Sweeten as desired, and serve over ice.

2 teaspoons minced fresh ginger

2 tablespoons loose-leaf rooibos tea (or 6 tea bags)

Raw honey or pure maple syrup (optional)

ROOIBOS Rooibos tea, or red bush tea, is made from the oxidized leaves of a small shrub that grows exclusively in the Western Cape province of South Africa. Not only is rooibos delicious, it also had many health benefits. Rooibos leaves are high in antioxidants and essential minerals and have been officially recognized as a leading source of natural anticarcinogenic compounds. I really like rooibos tea because it is caffeine-free, making it perfect for pregnant and breastfeeding women and even children. Combining rooibos with ginger creates a fantastic tonic for improving digestion.

MULTIGRAIN CARROT CAKE PORRIDGE WITH PECAN CRUNCH

Who wouldn't want to eat carrot cake for breakfast? This bowl of heaven is simple, quick to make, and a totally sweet way to start your day. Although it isn't completely necessary, I highly recommend soaking the grains overnight to improve their digestibility. It also means that when you wake up, all you have to do is throw in your favorite additions and sit down to a healthy morning meal that tastes like a serious indulgence. The pecan crunch really makes this breakfast special, but it can be used to gussy up anything from a modest bowl of oats to a fancy dessert!

To make things easier, use just water instead of carrot juice to soak the grains. You can also make a double or triple batch and keep it in the fridge for up to three days, stored in a tightly sealed container.

1 cup / 100g combination of rolled grains (oat, rye, spelt, emmer . . .), soaked, if possible (soak for a minimum of 8 hours)

½ teaspoon freshly squeezed lemon juice

1¼ cups / 280 ml carrot juice or water, or more if needed

⅓ cup / 30g grated carrot

Pinch of fine sea salt

Generous pinch of ground cinnamon

Generous pinch of ginger

Generous pinch of nutmeg

Generous pinch of cloves

Generous pinch of cardamom

Handful of raisins or other dried fruit (chopped dates, pineapple, apricots . . .)

⅓ cup / 20g unsweetened flaked coconut

6 to 8 tablespoons pecan crunch (recipe follows), to taste

2 dollops goat or sheep yogurt (optional)

Pure maple syrup (optional)

1. Combine the grains, lemon juice, and carrot juice in a jar or bowl. Let rest, covered, in the fridge overnight.

2. In the morning, remove the jar from the fridge; let it stand at room temperature for 15 minutes to warm up slightly if desired. (You can also eat the grains warm. Simply put the grains in a pot and heat gently on the stove until they are to your liking. Just don't boil the grains, as they are full of heat-sensitive enzymes.) Fold in the grated carrots, salt, spices, raisins, and coconut flakes. Add more carrot juice or water if desired. Top each serving with pecan crunch, a dollop of yogurt, and a drizzle of maple syrup, if desired.

CARROTS Carrots may seem humble, but they are one of the best dietary sources of beta-carotene on the planet. Beta-carotene functions as an antioxidant and an anti-inflammatory nutrient. When consumed on a regular basis, beta-carotene can help reduce the risk of developing many cancers by as much as 70%. The high fiber content of carrots helps to reduce the low-density (LDL, "bad") cholesterol and raise the high-density (HDL, "good") cholesterol, which is an important precautionary step against heart disease.

PECAN CRUNCH

MAKES 2 CUPS / 340 GRAMS 🟢 gf

⅓ cup / 80ml brown rice syrup

½ teaspoon ground ginger

2 pinches fine sea salt

1 cup / 140g pecans or walnuts, chopped

1. Preheat the oven to 350°F / 180°C. Line a baking sheet with parchment paper.

2. In a small saucepan, heat the barley malt over medium-low heat until it is runny. Then whisk in the ginger and salt. Add the pecans and stir to coat.

3. Spread the coated pecans out on the prepared baking sheet, and bake for 10 minutes. Remove from the oven, let cool completely, and then break into small pieces. Store in the freezer for up to 1 month.

TEMPEH MUSHROOM BREAKFAST BOWL

SERVES 4

Although I almost always lean toward the sweet side to start my day, I also love a savory breakfast when done right. This breakfast bowl is totally satisfying and energizing, and it makes a wonderful weekend morning meal. The tempeh is rich and meaty thanks to its amazing glaze, while the millet keeps things light and balanced. You can use any grain you like here; in fact, I often just use leftover grain I have on hand to save myself a step when my stomach is rumbling and I just want to eat! (This dish also makes a really nice lunch or dinner.)

2 garlic cloves, minced

1½ tablespoons minced fresh ginger

¼ cup / 60ml tamari

2 tablespoons pure maple syrup

2 tablespoons brown rice vinegar

9 ounces / 250g organic, non-GMO tempeh

1 cup / 195g millet, soaked if possible

Fine sea salt

2 knobs of coconut oil or ghee

1 medium onion, diced

½ pound / 250g mixed wild mushrooms, sliced

3 packed cups (¼ pound / 100g) spinach

3 tablespoons sesame seeds, toasted

Cold-pressed sesame oil or olive oil (optional)

2 medium spring onions, sliced, for garnish

1. In a wide, shallow pan, whisk the garlic, ginger, tamari, maple syrup, and brown rice vinegar together. Cut the tempeh into thin pieces and put them in the marinade. Let soak in the fridge for at least 30 minutes, or overnight if possible, flipping the strips every so often.

2. Drain and rinse the millet if you soaked it. Put it in a small saucepan, add ¾ teaspoon salt and 2 cups / 450ml water, and bring to a boil. Then reduce the heat, cover, and simmer until tender, 15 to 20 minutes (depending on your soaking time, if any). Let cool slightly with the lid still on, then fluff with a fork.

3. Heat 1 knob of oil in a large skillet over medium heat. Add the onions and a pinch of salt, and cook until they are softened and slightly golden, about 7 minutes. Add the sliced mushrooms and cook for 5 minutes without moving them (this will allow one side to caramelize). Stir and cook for another 3 to 4 minutes, until soft and browned. Pour about 1 tablespoon of the tempeh marinade over the mushrooms and stir to coat. Remove from the heat and immediately add the spinach. Stir until wilted. Remove the mixture from the pan and set it aside.

4. Heat another knob of oil in the pan. When it is hot, add the tempeh pieces and brown them on one side, about 5 minutes. Turn them over, add 1 tablespoon of the marinade, and cook for 1 minute. Sprinkle the tempeh with the sesame seeds, and remove from the heat.

5. To serve, spoon the millet into bowls, and then add a heap of the mushroom-spinach blend and a few strips of tempeh. Drizzle with sesame oil if desired. Garnish with the spring onions and add salt.

TEMPEH Tempeh (pronounced TEM-pay) is quite the ingenious little treat, made from whole soybeans and typically rice. Tempeh is much higher in fiber than other soy products because it includes the whole soybean. It is also higher in protein and contains more vitamins than tofu and is easier to digest because it is fermented. This means it is also a good source of gut-lovin' probiotic bacteria. Tempeh's flavor is often described as nutty, smoky, or like a mushroom, making it the perfect substitute for meat in classics like casseroles, stews, chili, and stir-fries.

BAKING WITH BEANS Looking to boost
the fiber and protein content of your baked
goods? Add beans! No, seriously. With
their mild flavor and incredible creaminess,
adding anything from pureed butter beans
to chickpeas in your favorite cake, cookie,
and muffin recipe will keep you fuller for
longer and will stabilize your blood sugar.
In general, you can substitute 1 cup / 180g
of cooked beans for 1 cup / 120g of flour.

FULLY LOADED BREAKFAST BARS

MAKES 10 LARGE BARS

There are plenty of premade convenience breakfast bars, cookies, and pastries on grocery store shelves these days, but if we look past the highfalutin' health claims and go straight to the ingredient list, are they really doing us any favors? It's time to ditch the plastic packaging and make your own handy breakfast-to-go. These insanely delicious bars are loaded with whole-food fiber, protein, healthy fats, real fruit, and even beans. Yes, it's true, and they still taste great! Perfect for kids, and for the kid in us all, so make a batch or a double batch, store them in the freezer, and have something to look forward to every single morning.

1. Preheat the oven to 350°F / 180°C. Line a baking sheet with parchment paper and set it aside.

2. Combine the chia seeds with 3 tablespoons water in a small bowl, and set aside for 15 minutes to gel.

3. Pulse 1¼ cups / 125g of the oats in a food processor until they resemble a very rough flour. Transfer the flour to a large mixing bowl and whisk in the remaining 2 cups / 200kg oats, baking powder, baking soda, cinnamon, and salt.

4. Pulse the beans with the coconut oil in the food processor until the mixture is creamy. Add the maple syrup, orange zest, chia gel, applesauce, and vanilla extract, and pulse until smooth.

5. Pour the bean puree over the oats mixture and stir until everything starts to come together. Add the apricots, raisins, pumpkin seeds, and cornflakes and stir to combine—you may need to use your hands at this point.

6. Shape the dough into 10 equal balls, and then flatten each one into a patty shape. Transfer them to the prepared baking sheet. Bake for 15 to 18 minutes, until the bars are golden. Let cool completely before enjoying. The bars can be stored in an airtight container at room temperature for 1 week, or in the freezer for up to 1 month.

1 tablespoon chia seeds

3¼ cups / 325g gluten-free rolled oats

1 teaspoon baking powder

1 teaspoon baking soda

2 teaspoons ground cinnamon

1 teaspoon fine sea salt

1½ cups / 250g cooked white beans, such as navy, white kidney, or Great Northern (about one 15-ounce / 250g can)

¼ cup / 60ml coconut oil, melted

¼ cup / 60ml pure maple syrup or raw honey

Grated zest of 1 organic orange

¼ cup / 60g unsweetened applesauce

1 teaspoon vanilla extract

⅓ cup / 70g chopped unsulfured dried apricots

¼ cup / 30g raisins

¼ cup / 35g pumpkin seeds

2 cups / 60g organic, non-GMO cornflakes (optional)

SORREL HUMMUS

MAKES ABOUT 1½ CUPS / 375ML

The first time I tasted sorrel, I was working on an organic farm in Northern California. The owner, giving me a tour of the property on my first day, bent down to pick a leaf and asked me to taste it. Upon trying it, I exclaimed, "It's like biting into a lemon!" That was the beginning of my love affair with this delectable little leaf.

Seeing as I love an extra-lemony flavor in my hummus, I knew that the acidic hit of sorrel would be an unexpectedly delicious addition to my favorite dip. The flavor is so bright, clean, and fresh, and just gazing at its vibrant green visage makes me feel healthier.

2 garlic cloves

1½ ounces / 50g small sorrel leaves, roughly chopped

1½ cups / 250g cooked chickpeas (about one 15-ounce/250g can)

¼ cup / 60ml tahini

Grated zest of 1 organic lemon

1½ tablespoons freshly squeezed lemon juice

½ teaspoon fine sea salt, plus more if desired

1½ teaspoons raw honey or pure maple syrup

Cold-pressed olive oil, for serving

1. Put the garlic in a food processor and pulse to mince. Add the sorrel, chickpeas, tahini, lemon zest and juice, salt, honey, and ¼ cup / 56ml water, and blend on the highest setting until smooth. Season with more salt if needed.

2. Transfer the hummus to a serving bowl, drizzle olive oil over the top, and serve. Store any leftovers in an airtight container in the fridge for 3 to 4 days.

SORREL Did you know that sorrel has the same powerful antioxidants and healing properties as kale? It also contains good amounts of vitamin C, fiber, iron, magnesium, and zinc. Sorrel is wonderful mixed with other salad greens and used as a seasoning in soups, casseroles, and omelets. Growing sorrel is very easy at home, even in containers. If you don't have any outdoor space for it, look for sorrel at farmers' markets and gourmet grocery stores from early spring through early summer. It resembles spinach, but one taste and you will know it's something entirely different! Choose sorrel with small leaves, as the young ones are tender and have the best flavor.

LABNEH WITH ROSE PETALS, SESAME, AND HONEY

MAKES 1 TO 2 CUPS / 250 TO 500ML
(DEPENDING ON THE WATER CONTENT OF YOUR YOGURT) ⓖ ☾

I love simple kitchen tricks—effortless processes that transform humble foods into special fare. Straining yogurt to make labneh, a Middle Eastern yogurt cheese, is one of those techniques. I started making this labneh on an early summer evening. The next morning, while the yogurt was draining, I went out for a walk and stopped to smell the roses that were blooming by the beach. Their shocking-pink color and subtle floral scent convinced me that they would be the perfect pairing with the cheese forming in the fridge. I picked a handful of petals, went home, and stirred them into the incredibly thick, tangy cheese along with some lightly roasted sesame seeds and golden honey. Complicated? Definitely not. Impressive? Most definitely.

Serve this labneh drizzled with raw honey on crusty bread, fresh vegetables, or even with oats in the morning. For a delicious savory labneh, drizzle the cheese with olive oil and za'atar (see page 44) or fresh herbs, such as mint, parsley, dill, or tarragon.

1. Line a large, deep bowl with a double layer of cheesecloth. Stir the salt into the yogurt, and then pour the yogurt onto the cheesecloth. Gather the edges of the cheesecloth together, tie with a string, and hang the yogurt over the bowl to drain (you can use chopsticks or a spoon across the bowl to suspend it). Put the whole contraption in the fridge and let the yogurt drain for at least 24 hours—the longer it drains, the thicker the labneh will be. (If you need to take a shortcut here, use Greek yogurt, which has already been partially strained.)

2. In a dry skillet over medium heat, toast the sesame seeds until they are fragrant and beginning to pop, 3 to 5 minutes. Remove from the heat.

3. Unwrap the labneh and put it in a bowl. Fold in the sesame seeds and rose petals. Drizzle with honey before serving. Store leftovers in a tightly sealed glass container in the fridge for up to 5 days.

¼ teaspoon fine sea salt

1 pound / 500g goat, sheep, or cow full-fat yogurt

2 tablespoons sesame seeds (black or white)

Handful of fresh wild rose petals (make sure they have not been sprayed!)

Raw honey to drizzle

GOAT AND SHEEP DAIRY
Goat's and sheep's milk (and the products made with them) are easier to digest than cow's milk because they have smaller protein molecules, and their proteins are the most similar to the protein found in human milk. In addition, the fat molecules in goat's and sheep's milk have thinner, more fragile membranes, half the size of those in cow's milk, which makes their milk easier to break down and assimilate in the human body.

CARROT TOP AND GARLIC SCAPE PESTO

MAKES ABOUT 2 CUPS / 500G

There is nothing quite like pulling carrots out of the ground, their bushy green tops standing at attention in all their freshness. But what to do with those lovely greens? I don't know about you, but I always feel bad tossing them away, so I came up with this delicious pesto that ensures you don't waste one bit of this veggie! Combined with garlic scapes, this pesto is rich, flavorful, and loaded with blood-cleansing chlorophyll. An unexpected and tasty twist on the familiar basil pesto, you can use this as a spread, a dip, or a base for dressings—or toss cooked grains and chopped veggies in its green goodness for a quick and easy salad.

1. In a dry skillet over medium heat, lightly toast the sunflower seeds until fragrant, about 5 minutes. Remove from the heat.

2. Submerge the carrot tops in a bowl of water and let soak for 2 to 3 minutes to remove any dirt; then spin dry.

3. Put the sunflower seeds in a food processor and pulse until they resemble sand (don't process too much, or you'll have sunflower butter!). Add the carrot tops, garlic scapes, lemon zest and juice, oil, honey, and salt, and blend on the highest setting until smooth. If necessary, add a little water to thin the pesto.

4. Store the pesto in a tightly sealed glass container in the fridge for up to 1 week. (It can be frozen for up to 1 month. Use ice cube trays and, once frozen, transfer the pesto cubes to a plastic bag with as much air removed as possible.)

½ cup / 70g sunflower seeds

2 packed cups / 65g carrot tops (leaves only—remove woody stems)

⅔ cup / 80g chopped garlic scapes

Grated zest and juice of 1 organic lemon

3 tablespoons cold-pressed olive oil

1 teaspoon raw honey or pure maple syrup

¼ teaspoon fine sea salt

CHLOROPHYLL Chlorophyll is essentially the blood of plants and gives leaves their green color. The molecular structure of chlorophyll is almost identical to that of hemoglobin, the oxygen-carrying protein in human red blood cells. This extreme similarity is what makes plants so darn good for us, and so beneficial to our health. Chlorophyll cleanses, oxygenates, and builds our blood. It helps detoxify and alkalize the body, and it provides us with antioxidants to neutralize free radicals. Chlorophyll is found in all green plant foods, but especially in dark green leaves, such as kale, Swiss chard, arugula, and, yes, carrot tops!

GRILLED ZUCCHINI AND GREEN ONIONS WITH BABY SPINACH AND HAZELNUTS

SERVES 2

The process of grilling is pretty miraculous to me. How can you take a relatively bland vegetable and make it taste amazing without adding to it or taking anything away—just grilling it? Perhaps it's the kiss of extreme heat that transforms the vegetable's sugars into something really special. Whatever the case, it's a quick trick that results in a complete flavor makeover. For a dish with so few ingredients, you'll be amazed at the complexity of tastes here. And even if you're familiar with grilled zucchini, the grilled spring onions will surprise and delight. The chile brings some heat, while the hazelnuts deliver an earthy, satisfying crunch. For a more substantial meal, add some crumbled goat or sheep feta, and perhaps some lentils or chickpeas.

1 medium to large zucchini

Knob of coconut oil or ghee, melted

Flaky sea salt and freshly ground black pepper

3 medium spring onions

½ tablespoon freshly squeezed lemon juice

1 tablespoon cold-pressed olive oil

½ garlic clove, minced

½ fresh chile, minced (Serrano is a good choice)

½ teaspoon raw honey

Grated zest of 1½ organic lemons

A few good handfuls of baby spinach

¼ cup / 35g hazelnuts, toasted if desired

1. Heat your grill (an indoor grill pan is fine as well).

2. Slice the zucchini lengthwise into thin ribbons (but not too thin or they will fall apart on the grill). Lightly rub melted oil on the zucchini slices, and season them lightly with salt and pepper. Slice and season the scallions in the same manner.

3. When the grill is hot, lay the zucchini and green onion slices on the grate, and cook uncovered until you have some char marks on the underside, 3 to 5 minutes. Flip them over and cook until tender and marked, another 2 minutes. Remove the vegetables from the grill and place them on a plate.

4. Whisk the lemon juice, olive oil, garlic, chile, honey, and grated zest of 1 lemon in a small bowl. Put the spinach in a serving bowl, and pour this dressing over it; toss to combine.

5. Roughly chop the hazelnuts. Arrange the grilled veggies on top of the spinach. Sprinkle with the hazelnuts and the remaining lemon zest, and serve.

ZUCCHINI Zucchini contains good amounts of fiber, potassium, folate, copper, riboflavin, and phosphorus, too. Summer squash's magnesium has been shown to be helpful for reducing the risk of heart attack and stroke, and combined with the squash's potassium, it can also reduce high blood pressure.

THE REAL DEAL GINGER ALE

MAKES 1 QUART / 1 LITER   ☾

I am about to put two words together that you thought you'd see only in your dreams: *Healthy. Soda.* It's true! Making your own authentic, naturally carbonated drinks out of simple ingredients, without any crazy colors, processed sugars, or preservatives, is totally easy and tons o' fun! Impress your family, dazzle your friends! This recipe is seriously phenomenal and you can do it. The instructions seem long, but they are quite simple. The two basic steps are

1. Make the starter, or "ginger bug" in this case—this is the culturing agent. Just like making a sourdough starter for bread, making soda requires a fermented substance that will inoculate the soda with friendly bacteria.

2. The second step is inoculating your drink of choice (fruit juice, herbal tea) with the fermented ginger bug, and letting it ferment. That's all!

It is highly advised, although not essential, that you obtain fresh organic ginger root for this project, as the skin of the ginger houses beneficial bacteria that will help the fermentation process.

GINGER BUG (SODA STARTER)

1 large piece organic fresh ginger

½ cup / 100g organic unbleached, unrefined whole cane sugar or palm sugar

FOR THE SODA

1 quart / 1 liter boiling water

⅓ cup / 40g minced fresh ginger

3 tablespoons raw honey or pure maple syrup

2 tablespoons organic unbleached, unrefined whole cane sugar

1. Make the ginger bug: Grate or finely mince 2 to 3 tablespoons of the ginger, leaving the skin on (if your ginger is not organic, peel it first). Put the grated ginger in a 1-quart / 1-liter jar, and add 2 tablespoons of the sugar and 1½ cups / 340ml unchlorinated water. Stir with a nonmetal spoon. Cover the jar with a piece of porous material (cheesecloth or a coffee filter will work) and secure the cover with a rubber band.

2. Over the next 5 days, stir the mixture at least once a day with a nonmetal spoon, and each day stir in 1 tablespoon grated ginger and 1 tablespoon sugar . Keep this mixture at room temperature. After 5 days (perhaps a couple days earlier and perhaps a couple days later), you should begin to see bubbles forming inside the jar; it will fizz a little when stirred and it will smell slightly of yeast.

3. Now you are ready to make your soda! Use 2 tablespoons of ginger bug for every quart/liter of liquid.

(RECIPE CONTINUES)

A FEW TROUBLESHOOTING TIPS FOR YOUR SODA MAKING

- Using sterile equipment is the key to successful bug and soda making. Use boiling water to kill all unwanted bacteria and then allow the equipment to air-dry.

- Friendly bacteria do not like metal, so do not use metal spoons, containers, or bowls to stir or store the ginger bug. Wooden, glass, or ceramic materials work best.

- Use only containers meant for carbonation, like glass flip-top bottles to store your soda. Other types of containers may burst!

- If you have been feeding your ginger bug for 8 days and you still do not see bubbles inside the jar, discard it and start a fresh batch.

- If mold develops on the top of your ginger bug, you can scrape it off and keep going. If you see mold twice, however, start over with a fresh batch.

- To make a constant supply of soda, keep your ginger bug alive by feeding it 1 teaspoon sugar and 1 teaspoon grated ginger every day and storing it at room temperature. If you know you will not be making soda, or know that you will not be around to feed it, simply put the ginger bug in the fridge and feed it once a week with 1 tablespoon sugar and 1 tablespoon grated ginger. To make soda again, bring the ginger bug back to room temperature.

- Test the soda every day for the desired level of carbonation. Once it is as fizzy as you would like it, put it in the fridge, where the cold environment will halt the fermentation process.

4. In a large heatproof bowl, pour the boiling water over the minced ginger. Cover, and let it steep for at least 15 minutes, until cooled to room temperature.

5. Once the ginger tea has cooled to room temperature, pour it into a 1-quart/1-liter flip-top bottle and stir in the ginger bug, honey, and cane sugar. Let the soda sit at room temperature, uncovered. During the next 24 hours, stir the mixture at least twice by closing the bottle and slowly turning it upside down and back upright again.

6. After 24 hours, seal the bottle and let it sit at room temperature for another 12 to 24 hours.

7. Taste the soda for fizziness—if it's lacking in the bubble department, seal and leave it out for another 12 to 24 hours. If you feel it is fizzy enough, put the sealed bottle in the fridge until ready to enjoy. The finished soda will keep for 2 weeks in the fridge.

VARIATION:
HIBISCUS LEMON GINGER SODA

Starting from step 3: Substitute ¼ cup / 12g dried hibiscus flowers for the minced fresh ginger. Add 1 tablespoon freshly squeezed lemon juice.

VARIATION:
ORANGE CLOVE GINGER SODA

This version is my favorite! Starting from step 3: Boil only 2 cups / 450ml water, and add 1 teaspoon whole cloves along with the minced fresh ginger. Once the tea has cooled in step 4, pour it into a 1-quart / 1-liter flip-top bottle and add 2 cups / 450ml freshly squeezed orange juice. Strain the cloves out before serving.

CARAMELIZED ONION, OLIVE, AND KALE CALZONES

MAKES 4 LARGE CALZONES

There are a few nights every summer when I dig out a fire pit on the riverbank at my cottage and make dinner by the water. These calzones were thrown together with late-summer leftovers from the fridge and cooked over an open fire. It could have been the perfectly calm river or the scrumptious smokiness from the coals, but these handheld pizzas became an instant hit with my family.

1. Slice the onions into thin rounds. Heat the ghee in a large skillet over medium-low heat, add the onions and a few pinches of salt, and stir to coat. Cook, stirring occasionally, and when the pan becomes too dry, add the balsamic vinegar. Cook until the onions are golden and caramelized, 20 to 25 minutes, or longer if necessary.

2. While the onions are cooking, remove any tough stems from the kale and slice the leaves into ribbons. Slice the tomatoes into quarters. Pit and roughly chop the olives.

3. Preheat the oven to 500°F / 260°C. If you have one, put a pizza stone in the oven to preheat.

4. Roll each portion of the dough out into a 10-inch / 25cm round on a piece of parchment paper. Sprinkle the dough generously with flaky salt. On one half of each rolled-out dough round, put about a quarter of the onions, kale, tomatoes, and olives. Sprinkle with the crumbled feta, oregano leaves, and black pepper. Fold the other half of the dough over and pinch the edges together, making sure the dough is sealed.

5. Slide the parchment onto a preheated baking sheet or a pizza stone. Bake the calzones for 7 to 12 minutes, until golden. Remove from oven, drizzle with olive oil, and serve immediately.

4 medium onions (about 1 pound / 500g)

A few knobs of ghee or coconut oil

Fine sea salt

2 teaspoons balsamic vinegar

1 small bunch (¼ pound / 125g) dinosaur kale

10 ounces / 300g cherry tomatoes

½ cup / 100g Kalamata olives

4-ingredient spelt pizza dough (page 95)

Flaky sea salt, for seasoning the dough

2½ ounces / 75g goat or sheep feta, crumbled (optional)

Handful of fresh oregano leaves

Freshly ground black pepper

Cold-pressed olive oil, for garnish

4-INGREDIENT SPELT PIZZA DOUGH

MAKES ENOUGH FOR 4 CALZONES

This pizza dough is amazingly simple to make and a very good recipe to add to your repertoire. Because it contains only four ingredients, it's easy to memorize, and you can use it to make pizzas, calzones, and flatbread.

1. Sift the flour into a large mixing bowl.

2. Dissolve the yeast in the lukewarm water, and then stir the yeast mixture and the oil into the flour. Continue stirring until you have a uniform texture, adding up to an extra cup of water, little by little, if needed (the dough should be moist but not wet, and workable with your hands). Start kneading by hand in the bowl or on a large, clean, lightly floured surface. Knead just until the dough is smooth, about 30 seconds—don't overwork it.

3. Dust the ball of dough with extra flour, cover it with a damp towel, and set it aside at room temperature for 1 to 2 hours, until it has approximately doubled in volume.

4. Divide the dough into 4 small balls. The dough can be kept covered for up to 8 hours at room temperature before baking. If you have any extra, wrap the dough tightly in plastic wrap and store it in the fridge for up to 2 days. Alternatively, wrap the dough and store it in the freezer for up to 2 months. Thaw completely before rolling.

3½ cups / 430g whole spelt flour, plus extra for dusting

1½ tablespoons active dry yeast

1 cup / 225 ml lukewarm water, or more if needed

3 tablespoons coconut oil or ghee, melted

SPELT Spelt, a grain with a five-thousand-year-old history, is experiencing a resurgence in popularity due to its wonderful taste, versatility, and nutritional content. Spelt does contain gluten, but gluten-sensitive people can tolerate spelt better than any other grain, as its gluten structure breaks down more easily than the gluten found in hybridized wheat (however, those with celiac disease must avoid spelt). It works just as well as standard wheat flour, and it offers higher amounts of protein and fiber and a broader spectrum of nutrients. Spelt also has special carbohydrates called mucopolysaccharides, which play an important role in stimulating the immune system.

FULL BLOOM ARUGULA SALAD WITH MILLET, RED CURRANTS, AND NASTURTIUMS

SERVES 2 TO 3

Could this salad be any more beautiful? There is nothing quite like eating flowers, especially when they are fresh from the garden. Many blossoms are in fact edible and surprisingly healthy; I use nasturtiums in this salad, which are plentiful from early summer through the autumn. I love this flower because one plant yields several different-colored flowers, from white to golden yellow and vibrant red, and the flavor is unmistakably piquant, adding a lively kick. But feel free to use any edible flower—just make sure that they have not been sprayed with any chemicals. The currants provide an incredible sweet-tartness here, and the pistachios add lovely crunch and nuttiness.

½ cup / 100g millet, soaked if possible

Fine sea salt

¼ cup / 35g raw pistachios

1½ tablespoons cold-pressed olive oil

1½ tablespoons white balsamic vinegar

2 cups / 50g arugula

Handful of fresh mint leaves, chopped

1 cup / 130g fresh red currants

8 to 10 nasturtium flowers (arugula flowers are also delicious in this salad)

1. Wash the millet well and put it in a dry saucepan. Toast the millet over medium heat for about 5 minutes, until it becomes fragrant. Add 1 cup / 225ml water and a couple pinches of sea salt. Bring to a boil, reduce the heat, and cover with a tight-fitting lid. Simmer until the millet is tender, 15 to 20 minutes, depending on your soaking time, if any. If the water is absorbed before the millet is fully cooked, add a little more as needed. Remove from the heat, let cool, covered, for 5 minutes, and then fluff with a fork. Put the millet in a large bowl and set it aside to cool completely.

2. In a dry skillet over medium heat, lightly toast the pistachios until fragrant, about 5 minutes. Remove from the heat and roughly chop.

3. Whisk the olive oil, vinegar, and a pinch of sea salt together in a small bowl, and pour half of this dressing over the millet.

4. Put the arugula in a large bowl, and toss in the mint, pistachios, and currants. Pour the remaining dressing over, and fold gently to coat. Add the millet and fold. Pull petals off some of the nasturtium flowers, leaving a few whole, and add both to the salad. Serve.

CARAMELIZED FENNEL ON HERBED POLENTA

SERVES 2 gf

I first made caramelized fennel by mistake. I was roasting some other vegetables, which were covered in a maple syrup–based glaze, on the same baking sheet, and some of the glaze ran onto the fennel . . . and tasted amazing. I had never thought about making fennel even sweeter than it is, but it was a delicious mishap that led to this recipe. The contrast between these two elements is truly amazing: the savory, creamy polenta against the chewy, sweet fennel. Use any herbs you have on hand, but a combination is lovely if you have more than one.

2 to 3 cups / 450 to 675ml vegetable broth, as needed

½ cup / 85g organic, non-GMO polenta

Fine sea salt

1 large fennel bulb

Knob of ghee or coconut oil

2 tablespoons raw fennel seeds

1 to 2 tablespoons pure maple syrup, to taste

¼ cup / 5g chopped mixed herbs, such as parsley, dill, and chives

¼ cup / 27g grated Pecorino Romano cheese (optional)

Cold-pressed olive oil

Herb flowers, such as dill, if available, for garnish

1. Heat the vegetable broth in a large saucepan until simmering. Slowly pour in the polenta in a steady stream, whisking all the while to prevent clumping. Add a few pinches of salt. Stir constantly for a couple minutes; then reduce the heat and simmer, stirring every 5 minutes or so for 30 to 45 minutes (read the label on your own box for cooking time approximations). If the polenta becomes too thick, add more broth or hot water and whisk it in until smooth. The polenta is cooked when you rub a small amount of it between your fingers and it is no longer gritty, but instead creamy and smooth.

2. While the polenta is cooking, cut the fennel bulb into thin vertical slices (from the top to the base).

3. Heat the ghee in a large skillet on medium-high heat. Working in batches, add the fennel slices to the skillet, making sure that they all come into contact with the surface of the skillet (not overlapping—you may have to work with a few slices at a time). Sprinkle with sea salt. Do not stir or move the fennel until it is golden on the bottom, about 5 to 7 minutes. When all the pieces have browned, flip them onto the uncooked side. When the underside has also browned, add a sprinkling of fennel seeds and ½ tablespoon of the maple syrup, and let cook for 1 minute. Toss to coat, transfer the fennel to a plate, and repeat until all the fennel is cooked. Season with salt if desired.

4. Add the chopped herbs and grated cheese to the polenta, and give it a final stir. Whisk in a little more broth or water to thin it if necessary.

5. To serve, scoop a portion of polenta onto a plate, then arrange the caramelized fennel on top. Add a drizzle of olive oil. Garnish with herb flowers if available.

FENNEL Fennel is one of my absolute favorite vegetables. It is crisp, fresh, and licorice-y, and fantastic both cooked and raw. I dig the fact that every part of fennel can be eaten, including the seeds, which are sweet and pungent. With a fantastic flavor-concentrated crunch, fennel seeds add anise-like sparks to salads, curried stews, soups, and grain dishes. Looking for a natural breath freshener? Chew on the seeds—they are delicious, and they really work. Fennel is a healing food, high in vitamins A and C. Its most intriguing phytonutrient is anethole, which has been shown to reduce inflammation, protect the liver, and prevent the occurrence of cancer.

THAI-STYLE COCONUT SOUP WITH ZUCCHINI NOODLES

SERVES 3 TO 4

This recipe comes from my friend Kiki, who can cook authentic Thai food like nobody's business. The first time I tried this soup, I totally flipped out—what looked like a bowl of hot milk turned out to be the biggest flavor bomb I've ever tasted. Although it is decidedly not Thai to do so, I add raw zucchini noodles to make the dish more substantial and give it some texture. When the noodles hit the hot broth, they soften quite a bit and become surprisingly tender.

The ingredients for this soup are admittedly special and require a trip to the ethnic grocery store, but it is well worth it. Lime leaves, lemongrass, galangal, and bird's-eye chiles can be found in most Asian markets.

1. Rinse the cilantro roots thoroughly and cut them off the stems. Reserve the tops; we just want to use the roots here. Trim the lemongrass where the white base portion ends; discard the tops, and pound the lemongrass bases until they are cracked and open. Peel the galangal, cut it into chunks, and pound it with a tenderizer until it releases a little liquid.

2. In a medium saucepan, combine the coconut milk, cilantro roots, lemongrass, galangal, shallots, chiles, coconut sugar, kaffir lime leaves, and garlic. Bring to a very gentle simmer; then cover and cook for about 15 minutes, until fragrant.

3. While the soup is simmering, prepare the zucchini noodles by slicing the zucchini into long, thin strips, with either a spiralizer slicer or a julienne slicer.

4. Strain the soup through a sieve into another saucepan; discard all the solids. Add the sliced mushrooms, lime juice, tamari, and 1 cup / 225ml water. Add more water if needed to achieve the right consistency—you want the soup to be light, but still creamy. Bring the soup up to a light simmer again, just to cook the mushrooms slightly, but do not boil.

5. To serve, put a handful of zucchini noodles in each bowl, and pour the soup over the top. Garnish with the enoki mushrooms, plenty of cilantro leaves, a slice of chile, slices of lime, and thinly sliced kaffir lime leaves.

1 bunch fresh cilantro, including roots

6 or 7 stalks lemongrass, to taste

1¾ ounces / 50g (about 1 inch / 2.5cm) galangal root or fresh ginger

2 (14-ounce / 400ml) cans full-fat coconut milk

3 shallots, sliced

2 to 4 bird's-eye chiles (also called Thai chiles), to taste, plus more for garnish if desired

2 tablespoons coconut sugar

12 fresh kaffir lime leaves torn into small pieces, to taste, plus thinly sliced leaves for garnish

4 garlic cloves, smashed

1 small zucchini

Generous handful white button mushrooms, sliced

4 limes: 3 juiced, 1 sliced for garnish

3 tablespoons tamari

2 handfuls enoki mushrooms, for garnish (optional)

FAVA BEAN, SWEET PEA, AND TARRAGON SOUP

SERVES 4

Fava beans are a delicious spring treat that is around for only a short amount of time. You can get frozen ones throughout the year, but there is something almost ceremonial about shelling the fresh ones yourself. A labor of love, yes, but it is well worth the effort. I really love fava beans paired with sweet green peas and tarragon, a sadly underutilized herb with a distinctive anise taste. This soup highlights the special flavors of both favas and tarragon, without their overwhelming each other. If you can't get your hands on fava beans, use all shelled green peas instead.

½ pound / 250g shelled fava beans (frozen are fine)

1 knob ghee or coconut oil

2 medium onions, chopped

Fine sea salt

3 garlic cloves, chopped

3 cups / 675ml vegetable broth

½ pound / 250g shelled green peas (frozen are fine)

1 small bunch fresh tarragon, to taste

1 tablespoon freshly squeezed lemon juice

Grated zest of ½ organic lemon

Cold-pressed olive oil, for serving

FAVA BEANS Fava beans, also called broad beans, are high in protein, complex carbohydrates, calcium, potassium, and zinc. Like other legumes, fava beans are full of both soluble and insoluble fiber, and more so than any other plant food besides wheat.

1. Fill a large bowl with water and ice cubes, and set it aside. Bring a large pot of salted water to a boil and add the fava beans. Boil for 2 minutes, remove them from the water, and transfer them to the ice bath. Once the beans have cooled, drain them and use your fingers to slip off the tough outer skin of the beans. Set the beans aside.

2. Heat the ghee in a medium saucepan. Add the onions and a pinch of salt. Cook for 5 minutes, until the onions have softened. Add the garlic and stir, cooking 1 to 2 minutes.

3. When the garlic and onions have softened, add the fava beans (reserving a few for garnish) and the vegetable broth. Bring to a simmer and cook until the beans are tender, about 10 minutes. Add the peas and cook for 2 to 3 minutes, until bright green.

4. Carefully ladle the soup into a blender. Add half of the tarragon plus the lemon juice and zest. Blend on high speed until completely smooth. Season with more salt if needed, and add more tarragon if desired. Serve immediately, with a drizzle of olive oil and the reserved beans scattered over the top.

AVOCADOS are loaded with monounsaturated fats—the good fats that lower cholesterol, reduce the risk of heart disease, and even offer protection against certain cancers, such as colon cancer and breast cancer. Avocados are also a concentrated source of the carotenoid lutein, a phytochemical that protects the eyes against macular degeneration and cataracts. Avocados contain significant amounts of vitamin K, essential for normal blood clotting; calcium, to maintain strong bones; folate, to combat against Alzheimer's disease; and vitamin C, to boost the immune system. Not bad for a handful of smooth green goodness.

MINT CHIP ICE CREAM SANDWICHES

MAKES 6 SANDWICHES

The fact that avocados and cashews can blend up into a luscious yet healthy ice cream is proof that the universe wants us to be happy! How can vegetables and nuts make ice cream? Well, let's not ask questions—just enjoy. Seeing as it is relatively difficult to hold ice cream in your hand, I decided to sandwich this delicious mint ice cream between thin, crispy chocolate and cacao nib wafers. You can enjoy them together, of course, but you can also just enjoy either of these things on their own. You'll win the lottery no matter what.

1. Drain and rinse the cashews and combine in a blender or food processor with the honey, avocado, coconut oil, peppermint oil, and ½ cup/112ml water. Blend on high until smooth. Taste for sweetness and minty-ness, and adjust to your taste. Pour into an airtight container and put in the freezer until frozen, 3 to 4 hours or overnight.

2. Remove the ice cream from the freezer about 20 minutes before assembling the sandwiches.

3. Put a scoop of ice cream on one cookie, then place another cookie on top, sandwiching them together. Roll the sides in cacao nibs, if desired. Serve right away or put in an airtight container in the freezer until you are ready to enjoy, or for up to 2 weeks.

1 cup/140g raw cashews, soaked for at least 4 hours

¼ cup plus 2 tablespoons / 75ml raw honey or pure maple syrup, or more if needed

1 small ripe avocado, sliced

2 tablespoons coconut oil, melted

14 drops food-grade peppermint oil or ½ cup (about 40 leaves) lightly packed fresh mint leaves, or more if needed

Raw chocolate cookies (recipe follows)

Cacao nibs (optional), for garnish

RAW CHOCOLATE COOKIES

MAKES 12 COOKIES, ENOUGH FOR 6 ICE CREAM SANDWICHES

1. In a small saucepan over low heat, melt together the honey, coconut oil, and cacao butter. Remove from the heat and whisk in the cacao powder and salt until smooth.

2. On a parchment-lined baking sheet, drop about a tablespoon of chocolate per cookie and let spread into a thin wafer. Sprinkle with 1 teaspoon cacao nibs. Repeat until you have 12 cookies.

3. Freeze the cookies until solid, then remove the parchment and store the cookies in an airtight container in the freezer for up to 1 month.

¼ cup / 60ml raw honey or pure maple syrup

3 tablespoons coconut oil

2 tablespoons cacao butter

5 tablespoons / 75g cacao powder

Pinch of fine sea salt

¼ cup / 30g cacao nibs

THE RAW BLONDIE

MAKES ABOUT 20 BLONDIES

Raw brownies are one of the most amazing and game-changing desserts I've ever made. Being a die-hard lover of this rich and chocolate-y dessert, I never could have imagined creating a totally raw version that was actually good for me. Once I had the recipe nailed down, I blogged about it, and people went nuts! This blondie is almost exactly the same as the now-famous raw brownie (without the cacao, of course), but I also kicked things up a notch and tossed in some of my favorite superfoods—lucuma, maca, and hemp—making these treats a seriously good-for-you food, full of protein, healthy fats, and antioxidants. What more could you ask for in a dessert?

2 cups / 185g whole raw walnuts

¼ cup / 40g maca powder

¼ cup / 40g lucuma powder

½ cup / 60g hemp seeds

½ teaspoon fine sea salt

2½ cups / 375g Medjool dates (about 18 dates), pitted

½ cup / 50g cacao nibs

1. Put the walnuts in a food processor and blend on high until the nuts are finely ground (do not overprocess or you'll end up with walnut butter).

2. Add the maca, lucuma, hemp, and salt to the food processor. Pulse to combine.

3. With the processor running, add the dates, one at a time, through the feed tube. What you should end up with is a mixture that looks rather like cake crumbs, but that when pressed will easily stick together (if the mixture does not hold together well, add more dates). Sprinkle in the cacao nibs and pulse briefly to combine.

4. Line an 8-inch- / 20cm-square baking dish with plastic wrap. Press the mixture very firmly into the pan so it holds together, especially around the edges. Chill in the freezer or fridge for at least 3 hours before serving (it is also easier to cut these when they are very cold).

5. Using a sharp knife, slice the blondie mixture into squares, and serve. Store any extra blondies in an airtight container in the freezer for up to 3 months.

WALNUTS Walnuts are my friend because I think they are the most delicious vegetarian way of getting omega-3 essential fatty acids. Why are they essential? Because your body can't make them, so they must come from the food we eat. I'd also like to think they're essential because omega-3s reduce cholesterol, lower the risk of heart attack and stroke, boost the immune system, control viral infections, improve brain function, and relieve symptoms of inflammatory conditions such as arthritis. No biggie.

MACADAMIA NUTS Macadamias are among the fattiest of all nuts, but do not despair! The type of fat found in these buttery little treats is monounsaturated, the kind associated with helping to lower the risk of heart disease, stroke, and breast cancer.

RASPBERRY MACADAMIA THUMBPRINT COOKIES

MAKES 16 COOKIES

Although these awesome little powerhouse cookies are in the dessert section here, they could easily be enjoyed for breakfast. Made with oats, honey, macadamia nuts, and raspberry chia jam, they are a simple yet rather complete treat. Macadamia nuts really make these melt-in-your-mouth delicious, but you can substitute any nut you like. The raspberry chia jam is easy to make, and if you have any leftovers, introduce them to a piece of toast tomorrow morning.

1. Make the jam: Blend the raspberries with the maple syrup in a food processor until smooth. With the processor running, slowly pour in the chia seeds and mix until they are fully incorporated.

2. Transfer the jam to a glass jar, cover it, and chill it in the fridge until it has gelled, 15 to 20 minutes. (You can keep the jam in the fridge for up to 1 week.)

3. Preheat the oven to 350°F / 180°C. Line two baking sheets with parchment paper.

4. Process 2½ cups / 250g of the oats in the (clean) food processor on high to make a rough flour. Pour the flour into a large mixing bowl, and stir in the remaining ½ cup / 50g oats, arrowroot powder, and sea salt.

5. In a small saucepan over medium heat, melt the coconut oil and honey together, whisking to blend. Add the vanilla and stir to combine.

6. Pour the wet ingredients over the oat mixture, and stir until just combined. Fold in the chopped macadamia nuts.

7. Using wet hands, roll the dough into balls, each about the size of a golf ball, and space them an inch or so apart on the prepared baking sheets. Use your fingers to create an indent in the top of each cookie, and spoon in enough jam to fill it.

8. Bake for 20 minutes, or until the edges of the cookies are golden. Transfer cookies to a wire rack to cool.

1 cup / 125g raspberries

½ tablespoon pure maple syrup or raw honey

1½ tablespoons chia seeds

3 cups / 300g gluten-free rolled oats

1 tablespoon arrowroot powder

1 teaspoon fine sea salt

⅓ cup / 80ml coconut oil

⅔ cup / 150ml pure maple syrup or raw honey

1 teaspoon vanilla extract

⅓ cup / 45g raw macadamia nuts, roughly chopped

PIÑA COLADA PASSION FRUIT POPSICLES

MAKES 10 POPSICLES

The first time I had a (virgin) piña colada was in Jamaica. I was thirteen years old and I thought I had died and gone to heaven. Something about the combination of creamy coconut and smooth, sweet pineapple hooked me, and when I returned to my nontropical life, all I craved was those two flavors. This summer, I re-created that incredible taste of the beach in a frosty popsicle. I added some passion fruit to the blend because it is tangy—almost sour—which contrasts so well with the mellow smoothness of the pineapple-coconut combo. Passion fruit also contains edible seeds that have a delicious crunch and look really beautiful suspended in frozen paradise.

8 medium passion fruit

3 cups / 375g chopped fresh (not canned) pineapple

1 (14 ounce / 400ml) can full-fat coconut milk

2 tablespoons raw honey or pure maple syrup

1. Scoop out the flesh from the passion fruit into a small bowl and set it aside. (You will have about 1 cup total fruit pulp.)

2. Combine the pineapple, coconut milk, and honey in a blender, and blend on high speed until smooth.

3. Into each popsicle mold, pour a small amount of either the pineapple-coconut blend or the passion fruit pulp, and then alternate between the two until you've almost reached the top (leave a small amount of space at the top to allow the liquid to expand slightly in the freezer). Using a popsicle stick or skewer, stir the liquids a little bit to create a marble effect.

4. Insert a popsicle stick in each mold, and freeze until completely frozen, about 4 hours.

5. To serve, run each mold under warm water until the popsicle easily slides out.

PINEAPPLE Pineapples are excellent for digestion because they contain an enzyme called bromelain. Bromelain is also a powerful anti-inflammatory and is widely available in supplement form. Pineapples work to cleanse the body, purify the blood, and increase circulation. Their key nutrients include vitamin C, folate, iron, and manganese.

LATE SUMMER

MORNINGS

RASPBERRY BREEZE SMOOTHIE

RAW CASHEW YOGURT WITH MAPLE AND BLACKBERRY

CORNMEAL PANCAKES WITH GINGERED PLUM COMPOTE

BLUEBERRY CARDAMOM CHIA PUDDING

SMALL MEASURES

SPARKLING MINT MELONADE

CLEANSING GRAPE SALSA

ZUCCHINI FIRECRACKER CORN BREAD

ROASTED RED PEPPER WALNUT DIP

HEIRLOOM TOMATOES WITH OIL-CURED OLIVES AND CRUSTY BREAD

SUNDOWN CARROT AND GRILLED CORN SALAD

THE BEST LENTIL SALAD EVER

MAINS

CBLT—COCONUT BACON LETTUCE TOMATO SANDWICH

CUCUMBER NIGELLA SPELT SALAD

MISO SESAME-GLAZED EGGPLANT

GRAIN-FREE HEMP TABBOULEH

BUCKWHEAT CREPES WITH CREAMY PURPLE STRING BEAN SLAW

SWEETS

BLUEBERRY-LEMON STAR ANISE CANTUCCINI

BERRY VOLCANO CAKE WITH WHITE CHOCOLATE HEMP SAUCE

RAW KEY LIME COCONUT TARTS

GRILLED PEACHES WITH BLACKBERRY SAUCE

RAWKIN' FUNKY MONKEY ICE CREAM

RASPBERRY BREEZE SMOOTHIE

SERVES 1 gf

Do you find yourself buying fresh herbs for a salad or some other dish and ending up throwing out half the bunch? If you're looking for an herbal use beyond a garnish, look no further than your blender. Mint, basil, chervil, lemon balm, and even tarragon are just some of the fresh herbs I've been known to toss into my smoothies from time to time. Not only do they add a totally unexpected flavor changeup, they contribute powerful phytochemicals and antioxidants, which protect the body against diseases.

Combine the raspberries, banana, mint leaves, hemp seeds, lemon juice, and nut milk in a blender and blend on high speed until completely smooth. Sweeten to your liking. Add more mint leaves if desired.

MINT The flavor of mint is familiar, sweet, and cooling—the perfect addition to a chilled smoothie on a hot summer day. Mint is a carminative herb, meaning that it is good for easing upset stomachs and toning the digestive tract. Mint is also helpful for relieving insomnia and nervous tension. To help break down fat, simply chew on some mint leaves—they help stimulate the flow of bile.

1 cup / 150g raspberries, fresh or frozen

1 frozen banana

Handful of fresh mint leaves, plus more for garnish if desired

2 tablespoons hemp seeds

1 teaspoon freshly squeezed lemon juice

½ cup / 125ml nut milk or water

Raw honey or pure maple syrup to sweeten, if desired

RAW CASHEW YOGURT WITH MAPLE AND BLACKBERRY

MAKES ABOUT 2 CUPS; SERVES 2 TO 4

If you really love yogurt but are trying to cut back on dairy, or just looking to change things up, this recipe is your new best bud. It is creamy, thick, and incredibly versatile—think beyond breakfast! I've made this yogurt with probiotics and without, and both methods work well, but the probiotic yogurt will ferment faster and contains more beneficial bacteria than the other. Whatever you add, your yogurt will turn out best if made in a high-speed blender, such as a Vitamix. You can use a regular blender, but the yogurt will not be completely smooth.

It's very important that you use nonchlorinated water for this recipe, since probiotics do not thrive in a chlorinated environment. To remove the chlorine from your water, see page 252.

1 cup / 150g raw cashews, soaked for at least 4 hours

1 tablespoon freshly squeezed lemon juice

2 teaspoons pure maple syrup, plus more for serving

Pinch of fine sea salt

1 vanilla bean, split lengthwise, seeds scraped out and reserved

1 cup / 225ml unchlorinated water, or more if needed

1 probiotic capsule, or enough to equal 20 billion active cells (optional)

Handful of blackberries, for serving

1. Drain and rinse the cashews and combine them in a blender with the lemon juice, maple syrup, salt, and vanilla bean seeds. Pulse to break up the cashews. With the motor running, pour in the water and blend until the mixture reaches your desired consistency (add more water for a thinner yogurt). Pour the cashew blend into a glass container.

2. If using, open up the probiotic capsule and empty its contents into the glass container. Stir into the cashew blend with a nonmetallic spoon.

3. Cover the container with a breathable material, such as cheesecloth or a tea towel, and place somewhere warm. The fermentation can take anywhere from 6 to 24 hours, depending on the temperature of your environment (a warmer environment will mean less time). The yogurt is ready to eat when there are tiny bubbles forming and it has a pleasant tangy-sour scent. Use a nonmetallic spoon to taste it—if you like the way it tastes, enjoy right away with a drizzle of maple syrup and a handful of blackberries, or cover with an airtight lid and refrigerate for up to 4 days.

FERMENTATION Fermented foods restore and boost friendly gut bacteria, increase vitamin content, and add enzymes, all while helping us to digest the food we eat. Not a bad deal, eh? It seems, however, that living in a bacteria-phobic world seriously limits the number of fermented foods available to us. So let's change that and make fermented foods at home, like this simple cashew yogurt, the raw cashew cheese (page 170), and the real deal ginger ale (page 90). You'll open up an entirely new world of health benefits and tasty delights.

CORN Fresh corn and milled cornmeal contain a whole host of vital nutrients, such as calcium, iron, magnesium, phosphorus, manganese, folate, vitamin C, and vitamin B$_1$ (thiamine). Corn is also a good source of dietary fiber. Yellow corn is rich in antioxidants, especially carotenoids such as lutein. Carotenoids are yellow and orange plant pigments, known for their association in the prevention of chronic diseases, including cancer, cardiovascular disease, and macular degeneration. When purchasing corn, make sure to buy organic, non-GMO whenever possible.

CORNMEAL PANCAKES
WITH GINGERED PLUM COMPOTE

SERVES 4 (3 SMALL PANCAKES PER PERSON)

I really love pancakes and corn bread, so I thought, why not combine the two? The texture of these pancakes is amazing: a little crispy around the edges with some tooth in the tender interior, unlike regular pancakes, which are just soft all the way through. This makes the compote all the more appealing, as its sauciness works well on the slightly savory cakes. The ginger adds a bright, sparkling spice without being overwhelming and complements the sweet plums so well.

1. The night before, sift the cornmeal, corn flour, arrowroot, baking powder, baking soda, and salt together in a large bowl. Whisk together 1/2 cup / 125ml of the milk, the maple syrup, lemon zest, and eggs in a medium bowl. Pour the wet mixture over the dry mixture and stir to combine, eliminating any lumps. Cover and refrigerate overnight

2. The next day, whisk in the remaining 1/2 cup / 125ml milk.

3. Heat the coconut oil in a large skillet over medium-high heat. Once the pan is hot, add 3 large dollops of batter to the pan and cook until golden on the underside, about 5 to 7 minutes. Flip the pancakes and cook until set. Repeat with the remaining batter until all the pancakes are made. Serve hot, with sliced plums and the gingered plum compote.

3/4 cup / 130g cornmeal

1/2 cup / 65g corn flour

1 tablespoon arrowroot powder

1 teaspoon baking powder

1/2 teaspoon baking soda

1/8 teaspoon fine sea salt

1 cup / 250ml milk of your choice (nut, seed, rice . . .)

2 tablespoons pure maple syrup or raw honey

Grated zest of 2 organic lemons

2 large eggs

1 1/2 tablespoons coconut oil, melted

Sliced plums, for serving

Gingered plum compote (recipe follows), for serving

GINGERED PLUM COMPOTE

MAKES ABOUT 1 1/2 CUPS / 375G

1. Slice the plums in half, remove the pits, and roughly chop. Put the plums in a small saucepan and add 1 table-spoon of the ginger, the cardamom, sea salt, maple syrup, and 1/4 cup / 56ml water. Cover the saucepan and cook the fruit for 5 to 7 minutes, until the plums are soft and syrupy. Add the remaining ginger, if desired.

2. Add more salt and/or maple syrup if desired before serving. Store any leftovers in a tightly sealed glass container in the fridge for up to 1 week.

12 medium plums (about 1 pound / 500g)

1 to 2 tablespoons minced fresh ginger

1/2 teaspoon ground cardamom

Pinch of fine sea salt, plus more if desired

2 tablespoons pure maple syrup, plus more if desired

BLUEBERRY CARDAMOM CHIA PUDDING

SERVES 1 Ⓥ ⓖⓕ ◖

The flavor of this pudding is outstanding—tangy, smooth, and sweet with a little kiss of cardamom that is sure to surprise! It makes a delicious breakfast, but you can also serve this as a dessert (as I often do). Although it tastes incredibly light, it packs a serious punch of protein, omega-3 fats, fiber, and stellar nutrients that will keep you feeling energized for hours.

I like using frozen blueberries because they make the pudding very cold and refreshing. If you have fresh berries on hand, just blend everything up and enjoy.

1 tablespoon chia seeds

3 tablespoons coconut milk

⅓ to ½ cup / 35 to 50g frozen blueberries

2 teaspoons freshly squeezed lemon juice

1 tablespoon pure maple syrup

Pinch of ground cardamom

1. Combine the chia seeds and coconut milk in a bowl. Chill in the fridge, covered, for at least 1 hour, until gelled; overnight is best.

2. Pour the chia-coconut gel into a food processor. Add the blueberries, lemon juice, maple syrup, and cardamom, and blend on the highest setting until smooth. Serve immediately.

BLUEBERRIES Blueberries rank at the top of the list when it comes to antioxidant-rich foods. Their anthocyanin content is extremely high; these are the nutritious, colorful pigments that give many foods their deep shades of blue, red, and purple. Happily, new studies show that freezing blueberries does not lower their overall antioxidant capacity or anthocyanin concentrations. This is wonderful news if you like to pick your own berries in the summer and freeze them, or if you can only purchase them from your grocer's freezer.

SPARKLING MINT MELONADE

SERVES 2

Would you believe that the inspiration for this recipe actually came from a slip of the tongue? I was trying to say "lemonade," but "melonade" was what came out. I realized how delicious that sounded and set out to make some! This is a super-refreshing drink to enjoy at the end of summer, when melons are ripe, juicy, and sweet. The flavors pair exceptionally well with lime and mint. With a little sparkling water, you'll feel as though you're sipping on a fancy cocktail while you're getting your daily dose of vitamin C, beta-carotene, and calcium. All you need to complete this treat is a comfy chair and a sunset.

You can use any melon you like for this recipe; cantaloupe (muskmelon), watermelon, honeydew, and Galia melons are all delicious and widely available.

1. Put the chopped melon in a blender, add the lime juice and honey, and blend on high speed until smooth. Add the mint leaves and pulse just to chop.

2. Fill a glass two-thirds full with ice, and pour in the melon mixture. Top with sparkling water, and stir. Garnish with more mint if desired. Serve.

MELON Melons are juicy, high-water-content fruits that bless us in the late summer and early autumn. They contain good amounts of calcium, potassium, vitamin C, and vitamin A as beta-carotene, especially in cantaloupe and watermelon. Because of their concentration of natural fruit sugars, they are digested easily, almost more than any other food. For this reason, it is suggested to enjoy melons completely on their own (or in this case, with just a little lime juice). This will help you avoid the fermentation that inevitably occurs when melons are combined with other foods, especially those containing protein and fat.

2½ cups / 250g roughly chopped ripe melon

1½ tablespoons freshly squeezed lime juice

2 teaspoons raw honey or pure maple syrup

Handful (about 20) fresh mint leaves, plus more for garnish if desired

Sparkling mineral water, to top up

CLEANSING GRAPE SALSA

MAKES 2 CUPS / 500ML

Cleansing seems to be a pretty trendy thing to do these days, as if it holds some promise of negating all the naughty things we've done to our bodies. As a nutritionist I will say that it is far better (and easier!) to be eating clean on a daily basis. This salsa is a perfect example of how we can enjoy delicious and cleansing food regularly without having to take any drastic measures: sweet grapes, tangy cilantro, and piquant chile team up to create a refreshing and detoxifying condiment. This is a tasty topping for crispy flatbread, grilled veggies, and, of course, tacos and baked chips. Try folding it into cooked grains. I also like to fill an avocado half with this salsa and go to town! After all, if we are going to behave, it had better taste wicked.

²/₃ pound / 300g mixed red and green grapes

1½ teaspoons minced fresh chile (Serrano is a good choice)

1 tablespoon freshly squeezed lime juice

1 teaspoon cold-pressed olive oil

2 tablespoons minced fresh chives

Fine sea salt

3 tablespoons chopped fresh cilantro

1. Slice the grapes into quarters or eighths, depending on their size (you want everything to be relatively small). Put the grapes in a medium bowl.

2. Add the chile, lime juice, olive oil, chives, a pinch of salt, and the cilantro to the grapes and fold together well. Season with salt. Let marinate for 30 minutes or so at room temperature before serving. Store any leftovers, covered, in the fridge for up to 2 days.

ZUCCHINI FIRECRACKER CORN BREAD

MAKES 10 TO 12 PIECES

Ka-POW! This corn bread is totally different from the one you're used to—it's chunky, spicy, and loaded with flavor! If you've got a bumper crop of summer squash on your hands, or if you just dig the idea of sneaking a few veggies into the golden corn goodness, then this is the recipe for you. This is a totally vegan version of corn bread—the protein and fiber-packed chia seeds act as the binder and are loaded with nutrition but are completely flavorless, allowing the other ingredients to shine through. I gave it the name "Firecracker" because it's colorful, spicy, and feisty! If you like your corn bread with a serious kick, use the full 2 teaspoons of red pepper flakes. If you've got kids at your table, scale back a bit or leave the red pepper flakes out completely. With the zucchini, scallions, and rich cornmeal, you'll still be certain to get some serious flavor fireworks.

1. Preheat the oven to 400°F / 200°C. Put a 9-inch / 23cm cast-iron skillet into the oven to heat up.

2. Mix the chia seeds with ½ cup / 112ml water in a small bowl and set aside to gel. It should take 15 minutes or so to attain the right consistency.

3. In a large bowl, sift the cornmeal, corn flour, baking powder, baking soda, salt, and red pepper flakes together.

4. In a separate bowl, whisk the milk, vinegar, coconut oil, maple syrup, and chia gel together.

5. Add the wet mixture to the dry, and combine in as few strokes as possible. Fold in the zucchini and scallions.

6. Carefully remove the hot skillet from the oven and put it on a heatproof surface; add the coconut oil and swirl to coat. Pour the batter into the skillet, scraping out any batter remaining in the bowl. Bake until the edges are golden brown and a toothpick inserted along the edge comes out clean, about 25 minutes. Let cool for at least 30 minutes in the skillet. Then slice into wedges and serve.

3 tablespoons chia seeds

1 cup / 170g organic cornmeal

¼ cup / 30g organic corn flour

1 tablespoon baking powder

½ teaspoon baking soda

1 teaspoon fine sea salt

1 to 2 teaspoons crushed red pepper flakes, to taste

1 cup / 250ml milk of your choice (nut, rice, oat . . .)

1 tablespoon apple cider vinegar

¼ cup / 60ml coconut oil or ghee, melted

1 tablespoon pure maple syrup

1 cup / 125g grated zucchini

3 scallions, sliced into rings

Knob of coconut oil or ghee, for greasing the pan

ROASTED RED PEPPER WALNUT DIP

MAKES 1½ CUPS / 375ML

Dips are an entire food group to me. I always have at least one on hand to spread on toast for a quick meal, to snack on with carrot sticks, or to use as a dressing in a grain salad. As much as I love hummus, I enjoy exploring the world of dips that use vegetables, nuts, and seeds as a base. This dip is particularly delicious in late summer, when the peppers are at their peak, but you can also make a decent version in the cooler months, as roasted bell peppers take on an incredible sweetness and depth of flavor. Complex and full of spices and tangy notes, the dip is delicious on everything . . . including a spoon if you can't find anything else! (If you want to increase the protein in this dip, add a handful of chickpeas, kidney beans, or lentils.)

3 large red bell peppers (about 1½ pounds / 700g)

1 teaspoon coconut oil

1 cup / 140g raw walnuts

1 large garlic clove

3 tablespoons cold-pressed olive oil

Grated zest of 1 organic lemon

Freshly squeezed juice of ½ lemon

1 teaspoon ground cumin

½ teaspoon smoked paprika

Pinch of cayenne pepper

½ teaspoon fine sea salt

Fresh parsley (optional)

1. Preheat the oven to 400°F / 200°C. Line a baking sheet with parchment paper.

2. Rub the peppers with the coconut oil and put them on the prepared baking sheet. Roast for 35 to 40 minutes, until blistered and blackened in a few places. Transfer the peppers to a bowl, quickly cover it with plastic wrap, and set the bowl aside for 10 minutes (this will steam the peppers, making the skin very easy to remove).

3. Reduce the oven temperature to 325°F / 170°C.

4. Spread the walnuts on a separate baking sheet and toast for 7 to 10 minutes, watching carefully so that they do not burn. Remove from the oven and set aside to cool.

5. When they have cooled, slip the skins off the peppers and discard them.

6. In a food processor, pulse the garlic until minced. Add the peppers, olive oil, lemon zest and juice, cumin, paprika, cayenne, and sea salt and blend on high until the desired consistency is reached—smooth or slightly chunky, whatever you prefer. Season to taste and garnish with the parsley before enjoying in your favorite manner.

BELL PEPPERS Did you know that green peppers are just immature red peppers? It's true! The first time I realized this was when I was working on an organic farm in Arizona. I picked a bunch of green peppers, thinking they were ripe, and the farm manager had a total bird. "Those needed another few weeks to ripen!" he said. And then he explained that the green ones were just immature red ones. I felt terrible, but I learned an important lesson, and why you shouldn't eat green peppers at all. It's difficult for your body to digest them because they aren't ripe yet. (This also explains why they are so much less expensive than their red older brothers.) Pass on green peppers from now on, in favor of red, yellow, and orange ones.

HEIRLOOM TOMATOES WITH OIL-CURED OLIVES AND CRUSTY BREAD

SERVES 4

This tomato salad is simple summer food at its best. It's incredibly quick to throw together and takes absolutely no culinary skill whatsoever, even though the flavors are rich and complex. With any dish containing so few ingredients, seek out the best quality you can find. Look for tomatoes in an array of colors, not only for aesthetics but also for taste. Farmers' markets are a great place to find heirloom varieties.

Oil-cured olives are a revelation for their mesmeric, meaty depth of flavor. Unlike plump brine-cured olives, oil-cured olives are wrinkly and rich—so much so that you need only a few of them to feel satisfied. The simple garlicky dressing just loves to be soaked up with some crusty whole-grain bread to make this a complete lunch.

1. Whisk the olive oil, vinegar, maple syrup, and garlic together in a small bowl, and season with flaky salt and cracked pepper. Let sit for 5 minutes for the flavors to meld.

2. Slice the tomatoes in halves or quarters, depending on their size. Combine with the olives and both types of basil in a large bowl. Pour the dressing over, and toss to combine. Season with flaky salt and pepper, and serve with slices of the crusty bread.

OLIVES Aside from being totally delicious, olives boast an astounding number of phytonutrients. Few high-fat foods offer such a diverse range of antioxidant and anti-inflammatory benefits, some of which are unique to olives themselves. And although they are a high-fat food, keep in mind that almost 75% of their fat comes from oleic acid, a monounsaturated, heart-healthy lipid. Key nutrients in olives include vitamin E, vitamin A, and many of the B vitamins.

2 tablespoons cold-pressed olive oil

2 teaspoons apple cider vinegar

1½ teaspoons pure maple syrup

2 garlic cloves, minced

Flaky sea salt and freshly cracked black pepper, plus more as desired

1½ pounds / 700g heirloom tomatoes

1 cup / 180g sun-dried oil-cured olives

Small handful fresh green basil leaves

Small handful fresh purple basil leaves

1 loaf crusty gluten-free whole-grain sourdough bread

SUNDOWN CARROT
AND GRILLED CORN SALAD

SERVES 2 TO 3

Farmers' markets are my happy place. This summer in Canada, I found the most beautiful carrots at my local market—deep purple on the outside, while the inside looked like a setting sun, fading from vibrant orange to a mellow gold. Seriously handsome. They inspired this Southwestern-spiced salad, because all they needed was a zesty dressing, a handful of herbs, and some heat. I decided to go all the way and added some grilled corn and cilantro, too. The smokiness of the corn paired so well with the sweet, crispy roots, and the dressing was out of the world. To make this more of a meal, toss in some black beans and serve it all over a cooked grain like quinoa or brown rice.

2 large ears fresh corn, husks
  and silks removed

Knob of coconut oil or ghee,
  melted

Grated zest and juice of
  1 organic lime

½ fresh chile, minced (Serrano is
  a good choice)

1 teaspoon raw honey or pure
  maple syrup

½ teaspoon sea salt

½ teaspoon ground cumin

1 tablespoon cold-pressed
  olive oil

3 medium purple carrots, sliced
  into thin rounds

4 medium spring onions, sliced
  into thin rounds

1 small bunch fresh cilantro,
  chopped

Smoked sea salt

1. Heat your outdoor grill or a cast-iron grill pan until hot.

2. Brush the corn with the melted oil, and grill until the corn is tender and slightly charred, 7 to 10 minutes. Let cool slightly. Slice the kernels off the cobs and put them into a large bowl.

3. In a small bowl, whisk together the lime zest and juice, minced chile, honey, sea salt, cumin, and olive oil.

4. Add the carrots, spring onions, and cilantro to the bowl containing the corn. Pour the dressing over, toss to combine, and let the flavors soak in for at least 10 minutes. Season with smoked sea salt, and serve.

THE BEST LENTIL SALAD EVER

SERVES 6 TO 8

Anyone who has eaten this salad will agree: it's simply the best. The list of ingredients may look long, but it's mostly spices, creating a combination of flavors for a totally addictive salad. It's picnic season, and this is perfect al fresco fare: it transports well, holds up for many hours outside of the fridge, and is a superb make-ahead dish.

The star of the show is the delectable du Puy lentil, revered for its ability to retain its shape and just a little tooth after being cooked. (Green, brown, and red lentils are great in soups because they are soft and tend to fall apart, but those would be less than perfect choices for this salad.) You can find du Puy lentils at any quality grocery store, natural food store, or health food store.

I like to use this salad as a base and add in herbs, greens, crisp veggies, nuts, and seeds and maybe some goat's cheese. Fold them in just before serving.

1. Rinse and drain the lentils. Put the lentils in a pot, cover with 3 to 4 inches / 7 to 10cm water, and bring to a boil. Reduce the heat and simmer, checking for doneness after 15 minutes. They should take about 20 minutes total; you will know they are done if they still retain a slight tooth. Overcooking the lentils is the death of this dish, so be careful!

2. While the lentils are simmering, make the dressing by combining the olive oil, vinegar, maple syrup, mustard, and spices in a jar with a tight-fitting lid. Seal, and shake vigorously to combine.

3. Finely dice the red onion. Chop the currants to make them a bit smaller than the onion dice. Chop the capers to the same size as the currants.

4. When the lentils are cooked, remove them from the heat, and drain them under cold running water to stop the cooking process. Once they have cooled slightly but are still a little warm, put the lentils in a large serving bowl and toss with the dressing. Stir in the onion, capers, and currants. Store leftovers in the fridge, covered, for up to 3 days.

2¼ cups (1 pound / 500g) du Puy lentils or black "beluga" lentils (do not use canned)

⅓ cup / 80ml cold-pressed olive oil

¼ cup / 60ml apple cider vinegar

1 tablespoon pure maple syrup

1 tablespoon Dijon mustard

2 teaspoons fine sea salt

2 teaspoons freshly ground black pepper

1 teaspoon ground cumin

½ teaspoon ground turmeric

½ teaspoon ground coriander

½ teaspoon ground cardamom

¼ teaspoon cayenne pepper

¼ teaspoon ground cloves

¼ teaspoon freshly grated nutmeg

¼ teaspoon ground cinnamon

1 medium red onion

1 cup / 140g dried currants or other dried fruit

⅓ cup / 40g capers

CBLT—COCONUT BACON LETTUCE TOMATO SANDWICH

MAKES 4 SANDWICHES

When I lived in Montreal, one of my favorite restaurants, Aux Vivres, was right around the corner from my house. Their best sandwich is the BLT, except the "bacon" is made with smoked coconut and tastes out of this world! I've never really been into imitating meat textures and flavors, but this stuff I'll make an exception for.

Whether you're vegetarian or not, you will completely fall in love with this CBLT. The recipe for the coconut bacon makes a lot more than you'll need for a few sandwiches, but once you've tasted it you'll find many uses for it. I love it on top of a salad (page 165), with eggs in the morning, crumbled on top of a stew, or on its own as a satisfying high-energy snack.

COCONUT BACON

¼ cup / 60ml tamari

1 tablespoon liquid smoke

3 tablespoons coconut oil, melted

¼ cup / 60ml pure maple syrup

½ teaspoon garlic powder

1 teaspoon freshly cracked black pepper

5 cups / 375g large unsweetened coconut flakes

SANDWICHES

8 slices whole-grain sourdough bread

Creamy topping of choice (mashed avocado, cashew cream, yogurt, mayonnaise)

Flaky sea salt and freshly cracked black pepper

4 ripe tomatoes, sliced

A few handfuls sprouts (such as sunflower or alfalfa)

Lettuce of your choice (mixed greens, romaine, spinach . . .)

1. Make the coconut bacon: Preheat the oven to 160°F / 70°C. Line a baking sheet with parchment paper.

2. In a large bowl, whisk together the tamari, liquid smoke, coconut oil, maple syrup, garlic powder, black pepper, and 2 tablespoons water. Add the coconut flakes and toss well to coat. Let the coconut marinate in the liquid for about 5 minutes.

3. Spread the coconut evenly on the prepared baking sheet. Bake for 20 to 30 minutes, stirring every 7 minutes or so, until fragrant, deep golden brown, and crispy. (The coconut will crisp up more outside the oven as well.) Let the bacon cool completely, and then store it in an airtight container at room temperature for up to 3 weeks.

4. Assemble the sandwiches: Toast the bread slices. Spread each slice with the creamy topping, and season with flaky sea salt and cracked black pepper. Add the sliced tomatoes, sprouts, and lettuce, and pack in as much coconut bacon as possible!

LIQUID SMOKE There aren't many applications for liquid smoke in my recipes, but to make coconut bacon, it's essential! Liquid smoke is made by collecting the smoke from burning fragrant types of wood, such as hickory or mesquite, in a condenser and cooling it until it forms water. The water droplets are then captured and filtered, resulting in a concentrated, smoky-flavored amber liquid. To ensure that you are buying a natural product, look for one with only water and smoke as ingredients—no flavoring agents, preservatives, or colors. Liquid smoke is available at gourmet grocery stores and some health food shops.

CUCUMBER NIGELLA SPELT SALAD

SERVES 4

Cutting a vegetable in an unexpected way makes it feel like an entirely new food. Take cucumber: instead of cutting it into rounds or small chunks, I sometimes turn the length of a cucumber into long, thin jade ribbons. Suddenly the texture changes, its appearance is unfamiliar, and it's more sophisticated.

To provide contrast with the silky, crisp texture of the cucumber, I use chewy spelt berries and creamy feta in this salad. Nigella seeds also add a special twist: with their nutty, peppery taste, they add sparks of surprising flavor to every bite. (Nigella seeds are also called black cumin, black caraway, Roman coriander, and kalonji; look for them at natural food shops and ethnic grocery stores.) This salad is simple, but lip-smackingly delicious. To make it even more substantial, add 1 cup / 165g of cooked white beans, such as cannellini, navy, or white Great Northern.

1. Combine the spelt, salt, and 2 cups / 450ml water in a small saucepan. Bring to a boil, reduce the heat, and simmer until the grains are tender and the water is absorbed, about 20 minutes. Put the spelt in a large bowl.

2. Whisk the olive oil, vinegar, lemon zest, and salt together in a small bowl. Pour half of this dressing over the warm spelt and toss to combine. Add the red onion and dill, and toss again.

3. Using a vegetable peeler or a mandoline slicer, slice the cucumber lengthwise into thin ribbons and add to the bowl. Pour the remaining dressing over the salad, toss to coat, and add the nigella seeds.

4. Crumble the feta over the top, gently fold, season with salt and pepper, and enjoy.

CUCUMBER Cucumbers are approximately 95% water, making them an excellent choice for warm-weather munching to keep our bodies hydrated. When eating cucumber, it is important to consume the entire vegetable, as the seeds contain the highest source of vitamin E of any plant and the skin is high in folic acid, vitamin A, and vitamin C. For this reason, purchase unwaxed cukes if possible, and don't scoop out the seeds!

SPELT

1 cup / 200g whole spelt berries

½ teaspoon fine sea salt

DRESSING

2 tablespoons cold-pressed olive oil

1 tablespoon white balsamic vinegar

Grated zest of 1 organic lemon

Pinch of fine sea salt

VEGETABLES

1 small red onion, sliced

1 cup / 20g chopped fresh dill

1 whole cucumber

2 tablespoons nigella seeds

1 small block (⅓ pound / 150g) feta cheese

Flaky sea salt and freshly cracked black pepper

MISO SESAME–GLAZED EGGPLANT

SERVES 2 **V** **gf**

One thing I really love about cooking is seeing how very simple ingredients can come together to make something extraordinary. This recipe is an excellent example of that—it's like magic. By taking items you may already have in your pantry—miso, vinegar, maple syrup, and tahini—and whisking them together to make a glaze, you end up with a surprisingly scrumptious treat.

2 medium Japanese eggplants

Knob of coconut oil or ghee, melted

2 tablespoons white miso

1 tablespoon brown rice vinegar

1 teaspoon pure maple syrup

1 tablespoon tahini

2 tablespoons sesame seeds

3 tablespoons minced fresh chives

Steamed rice for serving

1. Preheat the oven to 400°F / 200°C. Line a baking sheet with parchment paper.

2. Slice the eggplants in half lengthwise. Score the flesh on the diagonal and rub with a tiny bit of melted oil. Put the eggplant, cut side up, on the prepared baking sheet and roast until slightly golden and soft, 20 to 25 minutes.

3. Whisk the miso, vinegar, maple syrup, and tahini together in a small bowl.

4. In a dry skillet over medium heat, toast the sesame seeds until fragrant and popping, about 5 to 7 minutes. Remove from the heat and scrape the seeds onto a plate to cool.

5. Remove the eggplants from the oven, and turn on the broiler. Using a knife or spatula, spread the miso glaze evenly over the cut side of the eggplants. Sprinkle with the toasted sesame seeds. Cook under the broiler for 2 to 4 minutes, until just beginning to brown.

6. Put 1 eggplant (both halves) on each plate, sprinkle with the chives, and serve with a side of steamed rice.

EGGPLANT Eggplant is low in calories and virtually fat-free. The issue with eggplant, however, is that it acts like a sponge, soaking up more oil than you can imagine! The cooking method I've used in this recipe uses very little fat but adds oodles of flavor with the miso-sesame glaze, spread on and broiled briefly so the veggie is nicely roasted without being oil-soaked. The skin of eggplant is rich in potent antioxidants, so make sure to eat it up!

GRAIN-FREE HEMP TABBOULEH

SERVES 4

As much as I love traditional tabbouleh made with bulgur, this grain-free version is a tasty change of pace. Pulsing the chickpeas in the food processor chops them up into grainlike pieces and almost tricks you into thinking they are something other than beans! When they are combined with creamy hemp hearts, you won't miss the grains at all.

Instead of dicing the tomatoes, I use thick steaks of gorgeous heirloom varieties to showcase their unique shapes and colors. The mint and parsley are a breath of fresh air against the rich pine nuts and olive oil. Altogether this is a scrumptious, high-powered protein salad with an air of sophistication.

1. In a food processor, pulse the chickpeas until grain-size. Put them in a large bowl. Finely chop the parsley and mint leaves, and add the herbs to the chickpeas.

2. Toast the pine nuts in a dry skillet over medium heat until golden and fragrant, about 5 minutes. Immediately remove the pine nuts from the pan and transfer them to a plate to cool completely.

3. Add the cooled pine nuts, hemp seeds, sliced onion, and lemon zest to the chickpea mixture.

4. Make the dressing: Whisk the olive oil, lemon juice, garlic, honey, and salt together in a small bowl. Pour this over the salad, tossing to combine.

5. Slice the tomatoes into thick steaks and arrange them on individual plates. Drizzle with a little olive oil and sprinkle with flaky salt. Spoon the tabbouleh salad over the tomatoes, and serve.

HEMP SEEDS These are tiny cream-and-green-colored seeds that look a little like a round sesame seed. They have a mild flavor and an amazing creamy texture, which is delicious in salads like this one. To increase the protein and healthy fats in grain dishes, I often replace about 1/4 cup / 50g of the grains with the same amount of hemp seeds, adding a whopping 15 grams of protein to my meal.

SALAD

1 cup / 165g cooked chickpeas

1/2 packed cup / 20g flat-leaf parsley leaves

1/2 packed cup / 20g fresh mint leaves

1/3 cup / 45g raw pine nuts

1/3 cup / 45g hemp seeds

1 small red onion, sliced

Grated zest of 1 organic lemon

4 to 5 medium heirloom tomatoes (about 1 1/2 pounds / 700g) in different colors

Cold-pressed olive oil, for serving

Flaky sea salt, for serving

DRESSING

2 tablespoons cold-pressed olive oil

1 tablespoon freshly squeezed lemon juice

1 garlic clove, minced

1/2 teaspoon raw honey or pure maple syrup

Pinch of fine sea salt

BUCKWHEAT CREPES WITH CREAMY STRING BEAN SLAW

SERVES 4

The creamy yogurt dressing complements the tender-crisp beans, the walnuts add crunch, and the raisins give a touch of sweetness. The salad is delicious on its own, but I absolutely love it wrapped up in a warm buckwheat crepe. They are incredibly simple to make and elevate the entire meal to something special. This dish would make a delicious brunch, perhaps with an egg on top.

2 cups / 150g purple or green string beans

2 cups / 100g shredded cabbage

1 small red onion, very thinly sliced

½ cup / 125g goat or sheep yogurt

1 tablespoon Dijon mustard

¼ teaspoon fine sea salt, plus more if needed

½ tablespoon apple cider vinegar

1 teaspoon raw honey or pure maple syrup

1 small garlic clove, minced

⅓ cup / 40g golden raisins

½ cup / 70g raw walnuts, lightly toasted if desired

Handful flat-leaf parsley leaves

Flaky sea salt and freshly cracked black pepper

Buckwheat crepes (page 144)

1. Slice lengthwise down the center of each bean, creating two long halves, and put them in a large bowl. Add the cabbage and onion to the string beans.

2. Whisk the yogurt, mustard, salt, vinegar, honey, and garlic together in a small bowl. Add water to thin, if necessary, and then pour over the salad. Fold to combine. Add the raisins, walnuts, and parsley. Season with flaky salt and pepper.

3. To serve, put a crepe on each plate and pile it with the slaw.

PURPLE STRING BEANS If you are tempted to steam these purple beans, be forewarned: they turn green pretty darn quickly! The purple pigment in beans is the effect of their anthocyanin content. Anthocyanins are powerful health-promoting phytochemicals, but they are also water-soluble and extremely sensitive to heat. When boiled, anthocyanins deteriorate, leaving behind the still-good-for-you green bean, which is full of chlorophyll. Enjoying the purple beans raw, as in this salad, will ensure you are getting the full benefit of their anthocyanins while still enjoying their beautiful color.

BUCKWHEAT CREPES

MAKES 4 CREPES

½ cup / 60g buckwheat flour

1 large egg

½ cup / 125ml plus 2
    tablespoons milk of your
    choice (nut, seed, rice . . .)

1 tablespoon nutritional yeast

½ teaspoon fine sea salt

Knob of coconut oil or ghee

1. Sift the buckwheat flour into a bowl.

2. Whisk the egg, milk, nutritional yeast, and salt together in a separate bowl. Pour the mixture over the flour and whisk to combine, eliminating any lumps.

3. Heat a large skillet, and add a little oil. Once the oil has melted, pour in about a quarter of the batter and tilt the pan to form a thin coating over the bottom of the pan. Cook until the crepe becomes opaque and is no longer shiny; you should also see some small bubbles forming on the surface; this will take about 5 minutes. Carefully flip the crepe over and cook on the other side until set. Remove from the heat and repeat with the remaining batter, adding extra oil as necessary.

NUTRITIONAL YEAST Made from a single-celled organism called *Saccharomyces cerevisiae*, nutritional yeast is grown on cane or beet molasses, fermented, then deactivated with heat to stop the growing process. Because it is deactivated, it is totally unlike the yeast that you would use for baking and will not cause anything to rise—especially not your tummy! The natural color of nutritional yeast is a vibrant gold, and the flavor is often described as cheesy, which makes it a versatile and delicious substitute for dairy products in dressings and sauces. I sprinkle nutritional yeast on popcorn, salads, sandwiches, and soups and blend a little into hummus and other savory dips. Store it in a glass container at room temperature.

BLUEBERRY-LEMON STAR ANISE CANTUCCINI

MAKES ABOUT 25 COOKIES

As if you needed another excuse to curl up with a steamy cup-of-anything-hot this season, I'm giving you one: homemade *cantuccini*. And yes, by that I mean *biscotti*, sure. But in Italian, *biscotti* simply means "cookie," whereas cantuccini are the twice-baked biscuits we all know and love. (Hey, if I can't be a master Italian baker, at least I can be gastronomically accurate.) Eggs are a common ingredient in the traditional recipe, but I've made a vegan version by replacing the eggs with applesauce. The combination of blueberry and lemon is tried-and-true, but the addition of star anise gives these cookies a licorice overtone, which makes them taste unique.

1. Preheat the oven to 325°F / 170°C. Line a cookie sheet with parchment paper.

2. In a large bowl, whisk together the flour, baking powder, salt, and ground star anise.

3. In a medium bowl, whisk together the coconut sugar, applesauce, coconut oil, and lemon zest.

4. Stir the sugar mixture into the flour mixture. Add the dried blueberries and finish mixing with your hands.

5. With floured hands, shape the dough into three 3-inch- / 7.5cm-wide "logs," each about ¾ inch / 2cm thick, with the ends squared off. Place the logs on the prepared cookie sheet. Bake the logs for 25 to 30 minutes, until the edges are golden and the bottom is beginning to brown.

6. Remove the logs from the oven and let cool for 15 minutes. Then, using a sharp knife, cut them into ¾-inch- / 2cm-wide slices. Arrange the slices, cut side down, on the cookie sheet.

7. Bake the cookies for 5 to 10 minutes, until golden. Turn the slices over and bake for 5 to 10 minutes more, until golden.

8. Cool the cookies on wire racks, and then store them in an airtight container at room temperature for up to 2 weeks.

3 cups / 360g whole spelt flour

1 tablespoon baking powder

½ teaspoon fine sea salt

2 teaspoons ground star anise

1 cup / 120g coconut sugar

¾ cup / 190g unsweetened applesauce

1 tablespoon coconut oil, melted

Grated zest of 2 organic lemons

½ cup / 75g dried blueberries

BERRY VOLCANO CAKE WITH WHITE CHOCOLATE HEMP SAUCE

SERVES 10

This cake came to me in a dream: I imagined a volcano bursting with ripe berries and overflowing with creamy lava made out of white chocolate. (Obviously.) I had to make the cake in the waking world—and it is totally delicious all on its own: a moist, citrus-kissed cake with a hint of warm cardamom spice. If you want to leave it at that, go ahead—you will not be disappointed! However, if you want to go over the top and really take advantage of summer's brightest jewels, make the sauce, get some fresh berries, and go wild. The white chocolate hemp sauce is totally decadent but totally virtuous. Hemp seeds provide the body with essential fatty acids that will keep you feeling satisfied for hours. Drizzle this sauce on pancakes, fresh fruit, or breakfast oats, or put a squirt in your smoothie for extra yumminess.

2½ cups / 300g light spelt flour or other flour of your choice

2 teaspoons baking powder

1 teaspoon baking soda

1 tablespoon ground cardamom

½ teaspoon fine sea salt

6 tablespoons / 90ml coconut oil or ghee, melted, plus extra for greasing the pan

1 cup / 240ml pure maple syrup

1¼ cups / 300ml milk of your choice (nut, seed, rice, goat . . .)

1 vanilla bean, split lengthwise, seeds scraped out and reserved, or 2 teaspoons vanilla extract

1 teaspoon apple cider vinegar

Grated zest of 2 organic lemons

4 cups / 400g mixed seasonal berries, such as raspberries, blackberries, blueberries, and currants

White chocolate hemp sauce (recipe follows)

1. Preheat the oven to 350°F / 180°C. Lightly oil a Bundt cake pan with coconut oil.

2. In a large mixing bowl, sift together the flour, baking powder, baking soda, cardamom, and salt. Whisk to combine.

3. In a medium saucepan over low-medium heat, whisk together the oil, maple syrup, milk, vanilla seeds, vinegar, and lemon zest. Pour the wet ingredients into the dry ingredients and whisk to remove any lumps.

4. Pour the batter into the prepared cake pan, and bake until a toothpick inserted in the center of the cake comes out clean, approximately 1 hour. Let the cake cool completely before removing it from the pan.

5. To serve, put the cake on a large serving platter, and scatter the berries around it. Pour the sauce on top, slice, and enjoy.

WHITE CHOCOLATE
HEMP SAUCE

MAKES ABOUT 1 CUP / 250ML

3½ tablespoons / 50g cacao butter

½ cup / 75g hemp seeds

2½ tablespoons raw honey or pure maple syrup

½ vanilla bean, split lengthwise, seeds scraped out and reserved

1 tablespoon arrowroot powder

Tiny pinch of fine sea salt

1. Melt the cacao butter in a double boiler set over medium heat.

2. Pour the melted cacao butter into a blender, and add the hemp seeds, honey, vanilla seeds, arrowroot, salt, and ½ cup / 112ml water. Blend on high speed until completely smooth.

3. Store the sauce in an airtight glass container in the fridge. If the sauce solidifies, simply put the container in a pot full of simmering water to melt it again. Serve the sauce at room temperature.

RAW KEY LIME COCONUT TARTS

SERVES 6

Traditional Key lime pie is silky smooth, creamy, and rich, and so is this one. But would you believe that avocados are the star of the show here? Since they are a vivid green, I thought that flavoring avocados with fresh lime to become a tart filling would be just the ticket. Bingo: all the creamy qualities of avocados with the sweet-tart charm of citrus. The recipe for the filling is merely a guide, so adjust the amounts of sweetness and sourness to your liking.

1. Make the crust: Pulse the nuts in a food processor until chunky. Add the coconut, dates, and salt, and continue to pulse until the nuts and dates form a solid mass when squeezed together.

2. Line a 6-cup muffin tin with plastic wrap. Divide the crust mixture into 6 golf-ball-size portions and press one into each muffin cup, pressing up the sides as well, to create a tart shell.

3. Put the muffin tin in the freezer to let the crusts harden for at least 1 hour.

4. When you are ready to fill the tart shells, pull up the edges of the plastic wrap to remove the tart shells from the muffin tin.

5. Make the filling: Put the avocados, maple syrup, coconut oil, lime juice, and salt in a food processor and blend on the highest setting until smooth. Taste for sweetness and add more sweetener if necessary. If the avocados are overripe, add more lime juice to taste.

6. Spoon the filling into the tart shells and sprinkle the lime zest on top. Return to the muffin tin for storing and put in the freezer for at least 2 hours.

7. Remove the tarts from the freezer 15 to 20 minutes before serving.

LIMES Limes are loaded with phytochemicals, helping to boost our immune system, prevent cancer and atherosclerosis, and lower blood cholesterol and high blood pressure. They are famously loaded with vitamin C, one of the most important antioxidants in nature. Just ¼ cup / 56ml of juice delivers over 30% of your RDA for vitamin C.

CRUST

1 cup / 140g raw nuts (almonds and pecans are best), soaked for 8 hours if possible

5 tablespoons unsweetened shredded coconut

1 cup / 150g dates (about 7 large dates), preferably Medjool

A few pinches of fine sea salt

FILLING

3 ripe avocados, pitted, flesh scooped from their skins

¼ cup / 60ml pure maple syrup or raw honey, or more if desired

1½ tablespoons coconut oil, melted

¼ cup / 60ml freshly squeezed lime juice, or more if desired

2 pinches fine sea salt

Grated zest of 1 organic lime

GRILLED PEACHES WITH BLACKBERRY SAUCE

SERVES 4

Perhaps it's just the delicious anticipation, but that extraordinary, bright first bite of a ripe peach after waiting all year is like an epiphany. It is on those occasions that I feel pretty stoked to know that peaches are actually healthy, because I eat them like . . . well, like they are going out of season.

This recipe combines two of my favorite summer things: peaches and grilling. The trick is to scorch the peaches, getting just a slight hint of smokiness and caramelizing the outside while the inside still has that gorgeous, peachy tenderness. If you grill the fruit too long, they will get a little mushy, so keep a close eye on them. And as if the grilled peaches weren't delicious enough, I also made a wicked blackberry sauce to pour over the top, which I also love to cascade over pancakes, ice cream, yogurt, or even grilled veggies.

4 ripe peaches

Knob of coconut oil, melted

Blackberry sauce (recipe follows)

Raw cashew yogurt (page 116)

Raw honey (optional)

1. Preheat an outdoor grill or a cast-iron grill pan to high heat.

2. Slice the peaches in half and remove the pits. Rub each half with a little coconut oil.

3. Put the peaches on the grill, cut side down. Cook on high heat for 5 to 10 minutes, checking them every so often. You want to achieve some grill marks but not overcook the fruit. Inserting a sharp knife into the back of the peach will help you feel how cooked it is.

4. Remove the peaches from the grill and put them on a large serving platter. Pour the blackberry sauce on top, and drizzle with yogurt and honey if desired. Enjoy warm.

PEACHES The orange color of peaches is thanks to beta-carotene, the same phytonutrient responsible for giving carrots their pigment, as well as sweet potatoes and winter squash. Beta-carotene protects your cells from free-radical damage, which causes cancer, heart disease, arthritis, and other diseases related to aging. Beta-carotene is fat-soluble, meaning that it requires the presence of dietary fat in order for your body to absorb it. So rubbing the peach halves with the coconut oil ensures that you are taking in all that beautiful beta-carotene.

BLACKBERRY SAUCE

MAKES ABOUT ¾ CUP / 175ML

Put the blackberries, lemon zest and juice, maple syrup, cinnamon, and sea salt in a blender and blend on high speed until completely smooth. Sweeten with more maple syrup if desired. Store in a tightly sealed glass container in the fridge for up to 1 week. Serve at room temperature.

2 cups / 300g blackberries

Grated zest of 1 organic lemon

Freshly squeezed juice of
    ½ lemon

1 tablespoon pure maple syrup
    or raw honey, or more if
    desired

¼ teaspoon ground cinnamon

Pinch of fine sea salt

RAWKIN' FUNKY MONKEY ICE CREAM

MAKES ABOUT 1 QUART / 1 LITER

I really love Ben & Jerry's ice cream, especially their Chunky Monkey flavor, with banana, chocolate chunks, and walnuts . . . rapture! Setting out to make my own healthier spin, I had pretty low expectations. Nothing can compare to the real thing, right? Well, I am pleased to report that my totally raw version is pretty boss, and not just because it's good for you. Get creative with the cashew and banana ice cream base and add any kind of toppings. To mimic the original recipe, I toss in some cacao nibs and walnuts. This adds not only massive crunch and texture, but also a truckload of minerals, antioxidants, and omega-3 fats.

1. Soak the cashews for at least 4 hours, or overnight. Drain and rinse.

2. Peel the bananas and break them into chunks. Put the chunks in a plastic bag and freeze until ready to use, at least 4 hours. Remove them about 10 minutes before making the ice cream.

3. Combine the cashews and ½ cup / 112ml water in a blender and blend on high speed until completely smooth (this may take a couple minutes).

4. Slice the vanilla bean lengthwise down the center and, using the tip of your knife, scrape the seeds into a food processor. Add the frozen banana chunks, cashew cream, sea salt, maple syrup, coconut oil, and lemon juice, and blend on the highest setting until completely smooth. Taste for sweetness (remember that once frozen, the ice cream will not taste as sweet, so go a little sweeter than you would for a smoothie). Fold in the walnuts and cacao nibs. Pour into a glass or metal container and freeze for at least 4 hours to firm up.

5. To serve, remove the ice cream 5 to 10 minutes before enjoying—it's easier to scoop when it's a little soft.

BANANAS I could easily write an entire cookbook on bananas. They can imitate creamy dairy, substitute for eggs in baked goods, and make the best sweetener in smoothies. They are also one of nature's best sources of potassium, an essential mineral for maintaining healthy blood pressure and heart function.

2 cups / 280g raw cashews

4 very ripe bananas

1 vanilla bean

⅛ teaspoon fine sea salt

½ cup plus 1 tablespoon (140ml total) pure maple syrup or raw honey, or more if needed

1 tablespoon coconut oil, melted

½ teaspoon freshly squeezed lemon juice

½ cup / 70g chopped raw walnuts

½ cup / 75g cacao nibs

AUTUMN

MORNINGS

VANILLA ROSE APPLE CIDER

GREEN GALAXY SMOOTHIE BOWL WITH BUCKWHEAT CRISPIES

HAZELNUT FLATBREADS WITH MAPLE SPICE PUMPKIN BUTTER

WARM SPINACH, BACON, AND EGG SALAD

FIG AND BUCKWHEAT BREAKFAST TART

SMALL MEASURES

RED ONION LENTIL SOUP WITH MANCHEGO TOASTS

RAW CASHEW CHEESE

CELERIAC RIBBON SALAD WITH TOASTED CUMIN AND
POMEGRANATE

PAN BAGNAT WITH SUNFLOWER SEED TUNA

ROASTED BUTTERNUT SQUASH WITH GRILLED HALLOUMI AND
DUKKAH ON MASSAGED KALE

MAINS

SKINNY DIP WHITE BEAN FONDUE

ROASTED CAULIFLOWER WITH LEBANESE LENTILS AND KANIWA

FOREST FLOOR FLATBREADS

10-SPICE CHOCOLATE CHILI

ROASTED PUMPKIN WITH BLACK RICE AND TANGERINE
TAHINI SAUCE

SWEETS

PEAR APPLE BLACKBERRY CRUMBLE

CHAI SPICE UPSIDE-DOWN PLUM CAKE

WALNUT FIG BARS

RAW CHOCOLATE NIGHT SKY

BANOFFEE PIE

VANILLA ROSE APPLE CIDER

MAKES 6 CUPS / 1½ LITERS

When I am suffering from recipe writer's block, I get on my bike and go for a ride to the local market for inspiration. I come back with ideas and often a fun ingredient or two to play with. On one particular frosty autumn morning, I wanted something warming and special. Cruising the spice aisle of the market, I found dried roses, and a lightbulb flickered . . . Vanilla Rose Apple Cider! This beverage is beyond extraordinary—it's like drinking a thousand layers of petals infused with rich vanilla and sweet apples. It's complex, beguiling, and probably one of my favorite recipes in this book.

1. Slice open the vanilla bean lengthwise and scrape the seeds into a large pot; add the scraped pod as well. Pour in the apple cider. Heat the cider over low-medium heat until just starting to simmer. Remove from the heat, add the rose petals, and let steep, covered, for 15 to 20 minutes.

2. Pour the cider through a sieve into another pot or serving vessel, and reheat if necessary before serving. Store leftovers in a tightly sealed glass container in the fridge for up to 1 week. Reheat to serve.

1 vanilla bean

6 cups / 1½ liters apple cider (organic, cold-pressed, unfiltered is best)

⅓ cup / 4g dried organic food-grade rose petals

GREEN GALAXY SMOOTHIE BOWL WITH BUCKWHEAT CRISPIES

SERVES 1

Nothing is faster and more delicious than this meal-in-a-blender, and there is no better way to get a megadose of superfoods to help kick-start your day. In the warm months, I have a smoothie almost every day, either in the morning or as an afternoon snack. Kids love 'em, and adults feel as if they are eating dessert for breakfast. Everyone wins. Get as creative and silly with this as you like, making planets out of berries, stars out of bee pollen, and banana suns!

The other amazing part of this recipe is the apple-cinnamon buckwheat crispies, which have become a staple in my house. If you like to add a high-protein, high-fiber crunch bomb to your morning oats, fruit salad, or yogurt, these little buddies will surely satisfy. They also make a great snack to take with you on the go; make a double batch if you can, and snack on them beyond the breakfast table.

1. Put the banana, avocado, greens, and milk, plus any of your favorite additions, in a blender and blend on high speed until completely smooth.

2. Pour the smoothie into a bowl and top with the crispies and anything you like. To make the bowl look like a galaxy, add some fresh fruit slices, a couple berries, the bee pollen, plus a swirl of spirulina.

BLENDING YOUR FOOD Blending your food has so many benefits—it's not just for babies! For one, it's very easy to digest and assimilate liquids, as the chewing has been done for you. You can add a salad's worth of greens to a smoothie and not even notice, and it's the perfect way to use up leftover vegetables. Preparing and eating your food this way is super-fast, with nothing to cook and only a blender to wash. Try incorporating one blended meal into your diet just once a week to begin with, and work your way up slowly. If you feel a positive difference in your energy level and your digestion, maybe consider making one meal a day a blended one.

1 frozen banana

½ ripe avocado

Generous handful of greens
(such as spinach or kale)

1 cup / 250ml milk of your choice
(nut, seed, rice . . .) or fresh
juice

Handful of apple-cinnamon
buckwheat crispies
(page 160)

OPTIONAL ADD-INS

Handful of fresh berries

Fresh fruit slices

1 scoop plant protein powder
(hemp, sprouted brown rice,
pumpkin seed . . .)

1 teaspoon spirulina or chlorella

1 teaspoon bee pollen

1 to 2 tablespoons hemp seeds

1 teaspoon maca powder

1 teaspoon lucuma powder

1 tablespoon raw cacao powder

1 tablespoon chia seeds

APPLE-CINNAMON BUCKWHEAT CRISPIES

MAKES 3 CUPS / 450G

2½ cups / 460g whole buckwheat groats

½ cup / 75g sesame seeds

1 tablespoon ground cinnamon

¼ teaspoon fine sea salt

2 tablespoons coconut oil

½ cup / 125g unsweetened applesauce

3 tablespoons pure maple syrup or brown rice syrup

½ vanilla bean, split lengthwise, seeds scraped out and reserved

1. Preheat the oven to 350°F / 180°C. Line a baking sheet with parchment paper.

2. In a large bowl, combine the buckwheat, sesame seeds, cinnamon, and salt.

3. Melt the coconut oil in a small saucepan over medium heat, and whisk in the applesauce, maple syrup, and vanilla seeds.

4. Pour the wet mixture over the dry mixture and stir well to coat.

5. Spread the mixture out on the prepared baking sheet in a single even layer. Bake for 35 to 40 minutes, stirring after 20 minutes and then every 5 minutes or so, until golden brown and crisp (remember that the buckwheat will crisp up a little outside the oven). Let cool completely and store in an airtight container at room temperature for up to 1 month.

HAZELNUT FLATBREADS
WITH MAPLE SPICE PUMPKIN BUTTER

MAKES 15 TO 20 FLATBREADS

I always have food with me when I'm on the go. Whether it's an overseas flight or a bike ride downtown, I come prepared! Although these hazelnut flatbreads are a light and tasty breakfast, they are also the perfect snack to take with you any time of the day. I like to make a crispy sandwich with them, putting either sweet or savory treats in the middle: maple spice pumpkin butter, honey, tahini, cheese, thinly sliced veggies or fruit . . . get creative, be prepared, and never buy those packaged snacks from the corner store ever again!

1. Preheat the oven to 300°F / 150°C.

2. Spread the hazelnuts out in a single layer on a baking sheet and roast for 20 to 30 minutes, until fragrant and slightly darker in color (a good way to check is to bite one in half and check the color in the center—it should be golden). Remove from the oven and let cool completely.

3. Pulse 2 cups / 200g of the oats in a food processor until you have a rough flour. Pour the flour into a large bowl. Add the toasted hazelnuts to the food processor and blend on the highest setting until the nuts have a sandy texture (do not overprocess, or you will end up with hazelnut butter). Add the ground hazelnuts, as well as the remaining ¼ cup / 25g oats, the salt, and the baking soda to the oat flour.

4. Melt the coconut oil and barley malt in a small saucepan over medium heat. Add the liquid to the dry ingredients and mix well to combine—the mixture will be very dry. Add ¼ cup / 56ml water and stir to combine, using your hands if necessary. The dough should be moist but not runny—add more water if necessary. Let the dough sit covered at room temperature for 10 to 15 minutes.

5. Preheat the oven to 375°F / 190°C.

1 cup / 140g raw hazelnuts

2¼ cups / 225g rolled oats, plus
    more for garnish

1 teaspoon fine sea salt

½ teaspoon baking soda

2 tablespoons coconut oil

2 tablespoons barley malt

Coconut sugar (optional)

Maple spice pumpkin butter
    (page 162)

(RECIPE CONTINUES)

6. Divide the dough in half. Put one half between two pieces of parchment paper and use a rolling pin to roll it out into a thin rectangle. Remove the top piece of parchment paper, score the dough into rectangular or square shapes with a knife, and sprinkle with a few more rolled oats and some coconut sugar if desired. Keeping the dough on the parchment paper, slide it onto a baking sheet.

7. Bake for 8 to 12 minutes, until golden and crispy around the edges. Remove from the oven and let cool.

8. Repeat with the remaining dough. Break the cooled flatbreads into pieces, and store in an airtight container at room temperature for up to 2 weeks. Serve with maple spice pumpkin butter.

MAPLE SPICE PUMPKIN BUTTER

MAKES 2 CUPS / 500ML

½ medium pumpkin (about ½ pound / 250g; I used Hokkaido)

Knob of coconut oil

¼ to ½ cup / 56 to 112ml organic, unpasteurized, unfiltered apple cider, as needed

¼ teaspoon ground star anise

½ tablespoon ground cinnamon

½ teaspoon ground ginger

¼ teaspoon ground cardamom

¼ teaspoon freshly grated nutmeg

⅛ teaspoon fine sea salt

1 teaspoon freshly squeezed lemon juice

¼ cup / 60ml pure maple syrup

1. Preheat the oven to 400°F / 200°C.

2. Cut the pumpkin in half, remove the seeds, and rub the flesh with a little coconut oil. Transfer the pumpkin halves to a baking sheet, and roast until soft, 30 to 45 minutes.

3. Remove the pumpkin from the oven and let it cool; then remove the skin. Put the pumpkin flesh in a food processor, and add ¼ cup / 56ml apple cider, all the spices, and the lemon juice and maple syrup. Blend on the highest setting until completely smooth. Taste for sweetness, salt, and spice, and adjust accordingly. Add the remaining apple cider to thin the mixture, if necessary—you are looking for a creamy, thick spread. (Because pumpkin size varies so greatly, you will have to adjust the cider and spices to your liking.) Store in a glass jar in the fridge for up to 2 weeks.

WARM SPINACH, BACON, AND EGG SALAD

SERVES 4

Salad for breakfast? Skeptical? If you're a little wary of veggies first thing in the morning, this dish will surely make you a convert! I took the traditional bacon 'n' egg combo and put the whole thing on a bed of fresh greens and crispy sprouts. Instead of wanting to go back to bed after you eat, you'll be fired up, full of vitality, and ready to take on the day! As if you needed another excuse to make smoky coconut bacon, this meal is a great one.

1. Put the spinach in a large bowl, pour the dressing over it, and toss to combine. Add the sliced onion. Divide the salad among individual plates, and sprinkle with sprouts and the coconut bacon.

2. Soft-boil or poach the eggs, whichever you prefer. Put them on top of the greens, and season with flaky sea salt and cracked black pepper. Serve immediately.

SOFT YOLKS If you enjoy eating eggs, keep in mind that leaving the yolks a little runny when you cook them is a really good idea. The protein structure and many of the essential nutrients in eggs are heat-sensitive and are either denatured or destroyed by cooking the eggs into a solid state. Remember that purchasing organic, free-range eggs is your best bet for healthy, risk-free eggs.

4 to 6 large handfuls spinach leaves

Maple-mustard dressing (recipe follows)

1 small red onion or 1 shallot, sliced

Sprouts: broccoli, onion, and clover are good choices (see page 27; optional)

1 cup coconut bacon (page 134)

4 to 8 large eggs (1 to 2 per person, as desired)

Flaky sea salt and freshly cracked black pepper

MAPLE-MUSTARD DRESSING

MAKES ENOUGH FOR THIS SALAD

Whisk the mustard, maple syrup, sea salt, olive oil, and vinegar together in a small bowl. Season with salt.

2 teaspoons Dijon mustard

2 teaspoons pure maple syrup

2 pinches fine sea salt

2 tablespoons cold-pressed olive oil

2 teaspoons apple cider vinegar

FIG AND BUCKWHEAT BREAKFAST TART

SERVES 8

Dessert for breakfast—who's in? This tart is not just a showstopping centerpiece, but a delicious and nutritious way to start your day. It's the perfect thing to serve for a weekend brunch—it will impress all your friends even though it's a cinch to make, especially if you bake the crust a day ahead. Fresh figs are a sensuous treat, but because they are in season for only the blink of an eye, experiment with using any fruit you like in this tart. Strawberries in early summer would be dynamite, as would persimmons in the winter. You could even top the yogurt with stewed rhubarb in the spring. Yum!

CRUST

½ cup / 70g sunflower seeds

1¼ cups / 150g buckwheat flour

¼ teaspoon fine sea salt

¼ cup / 60ml coconut oil, chilled
    until very cold

2 tablespoons pure maple syrup

2 tablespoons ice water

FILLING

1½ cups / 350g thick, plain
    yogurt (such as Greek-style
    yogurt)

1 vanilla bean

1 tablespoon pure maple syrup,
    plus extra for drizzling if
    desired

5 fresh figs, washed and sliced
    into quarters

1. Preheat the oven to 375°F / 190°C.

2. Make the crust: In a dry skillet over medium heat, toast the sunflower seeds until golden and fragrant, about 5 minutes. Remove the skillet from the heat and pour the sunflower seeds into a food processor. Let cool for a few minutes, and then blend on high until the seeds resemble sand (do not overprocess, or you'll end up with sunflower butter!). Add the flour, salt, coconut oil, maple syrup, and ice water, and pulse until everything is well incorporated and the dough holds together.

3. Press the dough down very firmly onto the bottom and up the sides of a 7-inch / 18cm tart pan. Prick the crust all over with a fork, and bake for 15 to 25 minutes, until golden and crisp. Let cool completely.

4. Make the filling: Put the yogurt in a medium bowl. Slice the vanilla bean in half lengthwise, and scrape the seeds onto the yogurt. Add the maple syrup and fold to combine. Sweeten to taste with more maple syrup if desired.

5. Pour the yogurt mixture into the cooled tart shell. Arrange the quartered figs on top, drizzle with extra maple syrup if desired, and serve immediately.

FIGS Would it surprise you to learn that figs are in fact a very good source of calcium? Just 3 or 4 supply the body with over 100mg of this vital mineral. We know calcium is necessary for building and maintaining healthy bones, but it is also essential for supporting the functioning of muscles and nerves. Figs are high in fiber, both soluble and insoluble.

RED ONION LENTIL SOUP
WITH MANCHEGO TOASTS

SERVES 4

This is French onion soup turned into a meal! I absolutely love the classic version, but I find it rather pointless nutritionally, you know what I mean? I decided to take all that amazing caramelized onion flavor and toss in some lentils for protein, fiber, and added phytonutrients. I also included green anise seed, which delivers a sophisticated licorice-y touch. The best part of the soup, however, has got to be the melted cheese toast on top! I like to use Manchego, a sheep's milk cheese, instead of Gruyère. As it broils, the cheese becomes golden, bubbly, crispy, and completely addictive. The recipe calls for one toast per bowl, but trust me, you'll want to make extra.

1. Rinse and drain the lentils.

2. Slice the onions into rounds. Heat the coconut oil in a large saucepan over medium-low heat, and add the onions and salt, stirring to coat. Cook, stirring occasionally. When the pan becomes too dry, deglaze the pan with the vinegar. Cook until the onions are completely soft, golden, and caramelized, 20 to 25 minutes, or longer if necessary.

3. Add the bay leaves, thyme, anise seeds, lentils, broth, mustard, and black pepper. Bring to a boil, then reduce the heat and simmer until the lentils are tender, 10 to 20 minutes.

4. Mix the arrowroot with a little water so it becomes a thick paste; then add the arrowroot slurry to the soup, stirring well to incorporate it.

5. Preheat the oven to Broil.

6. Put the slices of bread on a cookie sheet, and put a slice of cheese on top of each slice of bread. Put under the broiler and cook until the cheese is bubbling and golden, 4 to 5 minutes.

7. Ladle the soup into individual bowls and put a piece of cheese-topped toast on top of each serving. Sprinkle some cracked black pepper over the top, and scatter a few fresh thyme leaves if desired. Serve piping hot.

¾ cup / 150g black lentils (du Puy lentils will also work), soaked for up to 8 hours if possible

5 large red onions (about 1½ pounds / 750g)

1 tablespoon coconut oil or ghee

1 teaspoon fine sea salt

1 tablespoon apple cider vinegar

5 bay leaves

5 sprigs fresh thyme, or 1 tablespoon dried thyme leaves, plus more fresh leaves for garnish (optional)

½ tablespoon green anise seeds

4 to 5 cups / 1 liter vegetable broth, or more if needed

2 teaspoons Dijon mustard

1 to 2 teaspoons freshly cracked black pepper, to taste, plus more for garnish

1 tablespoon arrowroot powder

4 slices gluten-free whole-grain sourdough bread

4 large slices Manchego cheese (Parmesan will also work)

RAW CASHEW CHEESE

MAKES ABOUT 2 CUPS / 500ML   ☾

Making a cheese out of nuts is actually quite simple, and all you need is a few basic ingredients to get started. Once you have mastered this recipe, feel free to experiment with adding different ingredients to flavor your cheese, such as fresh herbs, honey, dried fruit, citrus zest, or even edible flowers, for a beautiful presentation. This cheese doesn't firm up enough to be sliceable; its texture is more along the lines of a fresh goat cheese. Spread it on toast, savory crepes, or crackers; and serve it with olives, walnuts, and grapes on a cheese platter. Your friends will devour it without ever knowing it's totally raw and vegan!

2 cups / 280g raw cashews

¾ cup / 175ml nonchlorinated water

½ teaspoon garlic powder

1 teaspoon fine sea salt

1 tablespoon nutritional yeast

Grated zest of ½ organic lemon

1½ teaspoons freshly squeezed lemon juice

2 probiotic capsules, or enough to equal 40 billion active cells

3 tablespoons minced fresh dill fronds, plus more for garnish, or 1 tablespoon dried dill weed

1 tablespoon minced fresh chives, or 1 teaspoon dried chives

1. Put the cashews in a large bowl, cover with cold tap water, and let soak for at least 4 hours, up to 12. Drain and rinse the cashews.

2. Put the cashews in a food processor, add the nonchlorinated water, and blend on the high until completely smooth (this may take several minutes), scraping down the sides periodically. Add the garlic powder, salt, nutritional yeast, and lemon zest and juice, and blend again until fully incorporated.

3. Scrape the cashew blend out into a nonreactive bowl (glass is best). Empty your probiotic capsules into the cashew blend, and stir in with a nonreactive spoon. Fold in the dill and chives.

4. Cover the bowl with a clean dish towel and put it in a warm spot, such as on top of a radiator or inside a gas oven with the pilot light on. Your cheese will be ready in 12 to 24 hours (the time will vary depending on the temperature). Taste it: the cheese is ready when it is tangy and delicious.

5. You can mold your cheese by selecting a container that you like the shape of, lining it with cheesecloth or plastic wrap, spooning the cheese into it, and packing it firmly with a spatula. You can also roll the cheese into a log shape and then roll it in herbs or spices, such as cracked black pepper to create a distinctive flavor. Refrigerate, covered, for at least 6 hours before unmolding and serving. The cheese will keep for up to 1 week in the refrigerator.

CELERIAC Celeriac, sometimes called celery root, is a variety of celery cultivated specifically for its bulbous bottom. It is high in soluble fiber, which helps to lower cholesterol and may reduce the risk of heart attack. It is quite low in calories (1 cup / 150g contains only 42 calories; the same amount of potato contains 118 calories) and carbohydrates. All of this makes it a perfect food choice for those looking to keep their weight down. It is beneficial to the nervous, lymphatic, and urinary systems of the body. Key nutrients in celeriac include calcium to help maintain the acid/alkaline balance in the blood, iron for oxygen transport, magnesium to sustain bone integrity, and zinc to keep your immune system strong.

CELERIAC RIBBON SALAD WITH TOASTED CUMIN AND POMEGRANATE

SERVES 6

Entering the world of raw foods, I was unaware of just how many vegetables can be eaten without cooking them first. Beets, sweet potato, and butternut squash were just a few of my favorites that I thought absolutely needed the kiss of heat. Celeriac was another example: I'd always enjoyed its delicate parsley-like flavor in soups and stews, but until I made this salad, I had never served it uncooked before. What a revelation! When sliced thin enough and marinated in a little lemon juice, it is almost pasta-like, with a creamy and tender texture.

The salad is a surprising combination with the juicy pomegranate, crunchy almonds, and earthy parsley mingling in among the celeriac ribbons. Although small, the toasted cumin seeds deliver sparks of smoky flavor throughout. I also add a touch of orange flower water to the dressing, which tips the overall taste toward the exotic. One note: A mandoline is completely necessary for this recipe, no matter how good you think your knife skills are! If you don't have one, try a sharp vegetable peeler.

1. In a dry skillet over medium heat, toast the cumin seeds until fragrant, about 2 to 3 minutes. Set aside to cool.

2. Juice one of the lemon halves into a medium bowl of cold water. Slice off the gnarly skin from the celeriac, preserving as much of the vegetable as possible. Cut the head crosswise into ½-inch- / 1cm-thick rounds. Using a mandoline, slice the rounds into very thin strips. Drop the strips into the lemon water to prevent browning.

3. Roughly chop the almonds and parsley, and place in a large bowl. Add the pomegranate and cumin seeds. Drain the celeriac and add it, too.

4. Juice the remaining lemon half to make 1 tablespoon juice, and pour it into a small bowl. Add the olive oil, honey, orange flower water (if using), and salt and whisk together.

5. Pour the dressing over the salad, and toss well to coat. Season with more salt if needed, and serve.

1 tablespoon cumin seeds

1 lemon, cut in half

1 small head celeriac (about 1 pound / 450g)

½ cup / 70g whole raw almonds, soaked or toasted

2 cups / 20g fresh parsley leaves

Seeds from 1 medium pomegranate (about 1 cup / 180g)

2 tablespoons cold-pressed olive oil

1 teaspoon raw honey

1 teaspoon orange flower water (optional)

Pinch of flaky sea salt, plus more if needed

PAN BAGNAT WITH SUNFLOWER SEED "TUNA"

MAKES 4 SANDWICHES

When I was sixteen, I visited Marseilles, France, as part of an exchange program. The family I was living with was vegetarian, and since I wasn't really into eating meat that much myself, I gave their lifestyle a try. It seemed pretty easy and I didn't miss being a carnivore much . . . until we took a road trip to Nice, where I had my first *pan bagnat,* which is essentially a Niçoise salad in a sandwich: tuna fish, hard-boiled egg, veggies, herbs, olives, and crusty bread bathed in olive oil—in fact, that's how this sandwich got its name, "bathed bread." The combination made this new vegetarian weak in the knees. I ate it in front of my vegetarian hosts with a little bit of embarrassment, but a whole lotta pleasure.

Since that sandwich is practically vegetarian already, I came up with my own recipe for plant-based tuna. After soaking sunflower seeds for a snack, I realized that they had the look and texture of canned tuna fish—hence the sunflower seed "tuna" salad. The nori has that familiar taste of the sea, lending its fishy flavor to the seeds. Although pan bagnat is tasty right away, I like to enjoy this sandwich after it has marinated for a few hours, allowing the bread to soak up all that olive oil and delicious flavor. It's the perfect picnic meal or traveling companion.

SUNFLOWER "TUNA" SALAD

1½ cups / 200g sunflower seeds

1½ tablespoons plus ¼ teaspoon fine sea salt

2 tablespoons nori flakes, or 1 sheet of nori, finely chopped

2 tablespoons freshly squeezed lemon juice

2 teaspoons apple cider vinegar

2 teaspoons raw honey or pure maple syrup

2 tablespoons cold-pressed olive oil

½ cup chopped fresh dill fronds, or 1 tablespoon dried dill weed

2 spring onions, with tops, sliced

¼ cup / 30g capers

¼ teaspoon freshly ground black pepper

1. Make the salad: Put the sunflower seeds in a medium bowl, cover them with a few inches of water, and stir in the 1½ tablespoons sea salt. Set aside to soak for at least 4 hours or overnight.

2. Drain the soaked sunflower seeds and rinse them well. Put them in a food processor, and add the nori flakes, lemon juice, vinegar, honey, and olive oil. Pulse until you have a chunky paste, similar to tuna salad. Transfer the salad to a large bowl, and fold in the dill, spring onions, and capers. Season with the remaining ¼ teaspoon salt and cracked black pepper. (Any leftovers can be stored, covered, in the fridge for up to 5 days.)

(RECIPE CONTINUES)

SANDWICH

1 large whole-grain sourdough
  baguette

Cold-pressed olive oil, for
  drizzling

½ cup / 100g Kalamata olives,
  pitted

1 small red onion, sliced

¼ cup / 30g capers

1 large tomato, sliced, or a
  handful of cherry tomatoes,
  halved

1 red bell pepper, sliced

½ cucumber, sliced

Sprouts: radish, alfalfa, and
  clover are good choices (see
  page 26; optional)

Handful fresh basil leaves

Fine sea salt and freshly ground
  black pepper

3. Assemble the sandwich: Slice the baguette open lengthwise and drizzle the cut sides with plenty of olive oil. Spread half of the baguette with the sunflower tuna salad, and top it with the olives, onion slices, and capers. On the other half arrange the tomato, red pepper, cucumber, sprouts, and basil; drizzle with more olive oil, and sprinkle with salt and pepper.

4. Press the sandwich halves *firmly* together, and then slice into four portions. Eat immediately or wrap in parchment paper to enjoy later. This sandwich keeps well and actually gets better after it has marinated for a few hours.

SOURDOUGH Although pan bagnat is not traditionally made with sourdough bread, if I am going to eat bread at all, it better be fermented first! Sourdough bread is made by using a cultured starter, which helps the bread rise, instead of yeast. This has many benefits, the main one being that the longer rising time required increases the lactic acid of the bread, creating the perfect pH for the enzyme phytase to break down that unwanted phytic acid (see page 19). The lactic acid also slows down the rate at which the glucose is released into the bloodstream, actually lowering the bread's glycemic index. The protein gluten is broken down into its respective amino acids, making the bread far more digestible.

ROASTED BUTTERNUT SQUASH WITH GRILLED HALLOUMI AND DUKKAH ON MASSAGED KALE

SERVES 4

Butternut squash and halloumi cheese are a match made in heaven! Playing off the irresistible salty-sweet combo, this dish is one of my absolute favorites. Halloumi cheese has a distinct layered texture and a very salty flavor, but its most notable feature is its very high melting point, making this cheese uniquely grillable. You can also fry halloumi into crispy golden cubes for an addition to salads and warm vegetable dishes. Soooo scrumptious. This combination of sweet roasted butternut, salty halloumi, tangy kale, and nutty dukkah is perfectly balanced and completely addictive.

1. Preheat the oven to 400°F / 200°C.

2. Cut the butternut squash in half, remove the skin, scoop out the seeds, and chop the flesh into cubes. Mince the garlic. In a baking dish, toss the squash and garlic with a little melted coconut oil, and sprinkle with salt and pepper. Roast for 25 to 35 minutes, until tender.

3. While the squash is roasting, prepare the kale: Remove and discard the tough ribs. Roll the leaves into a cigar shape, and slice into ribbons. You should have 5 to 6 cups / 150 to 180g. Put the kale ribbons in a large bowl, and add a drizzle of olive oil, a little salt, and the lemon juice. Using your hands, rub the kale together, as if you were giving it a massage, for 2 minutes, until the leaves are dark green and tender.

4. Cut the halloumi into thin slices. Heat a grill pan or skillet over high heat. Add the halloumi slices in a single layer, and cook until grill marks appear (or until golden on the bottom if using a skillet). Flip the slices over and repeat on the other side.

5. To assemble, put a portion of the massaged kale onto each plate. Top with cubes of roasted butternut squash and slices of grilled halloumi. Garnish the entire plate with the chopped mint, red onion slices, a generous dusting of dukkah (or to your taste), and a drizzle of olive oil. Season to taste with salt if desired.

1 large butternut squash (about 3 pounds / 1.5kg)

2 garlic cloves

Knob of coconut oil or ghee, melted

Fine sea salt and freshly cracked black pepper

1 small bunch kale

Cold-pressed olive oil

Freshly squeezed juice of ½ lemon

1 brick (approximately ½ pound / 200g) halloumi cheese

Handful fresh mint leaves, roughly chopped

1 small red onion or 2 shallots, thinly sliced

Dukkah (page 179), for garnish

DUKKAH

MAKES ABOUT 1 CUP / 128G

Dukkah is an Egyptian nut, herb, and spice blend that is traditionally used as a dip for bread or fresh vegetables. Although there are many different versions containing a plethora of various ingredients, this is a simple version with hazelnuts, sesame seeds, coriander, cumin, salt, and pepper. I like to sprinkle dukkah on salad, grain dishes, avocados, and eggs—all delicious! This is a very easy thing to whip up and have on hand to liven up just about any meal. It's nutty, toasty, savory, and spicy. A jar of dukkah makes a great gift.

1 tablespoon coriander seeds

1½ tablespoons cumin seeds

1 tablespoon whole black peppercorns

1 cup / 140g raw hazelnuts

½ cup / 70g sesame seeds

1 teaspoon fine sea salt

1. In a dry skillet over medium heat, toast the coriander and cumin seeds until fragrant, about 2 minutes. Put the seeds in a mortar, add the peppercorns, and pound together with a pestle until pulverized (or grind in a coffee mill or in a food processor).

2. In the same skillet over medium heat, toast the hazelnuts until fragrant, 10 to 20 minutes (watch them carefully so that they don't burn). Transfer the hazelnuts to a plate to cool, and when they are cool enough to handle, rub the nuts together to remove the skins. Put in a food processor. Next toast the sesame seeds until they are fragrant and beginning to pop, about 2 minutes. Let cool slightly. Add the sesame seeds to the food processor and pulse with the hazelnuts until a chunky texture results (do not blend, as you will end up with hazelnut-sesame butter!).

3. Empty the contents of the food processor into a large jar or bowl, and add the coriander-cumin mix and the salt. Taste, and adjust the seasoning if necessary. Store in an airtight glass container at room temperature for up to 1 month.

SKINNY DIP WHITE BEAN FONDUE

I was born in the wrong decade. I totally missed the fondue era! The idea of a group sitting around a bubbling cauldron, dipping magical food wands into the creamy depths, sounds like a pretty rad time to me. I felt left out, so here is my version for a healthier era.

This fondue is, of course, made with beans. It's vegan, full of protein and fiber, but here you can totally gorge yourself and not feel as if you've done your body a disservice. I use nutritional yeast to make it taste a little cheesy, and miso to give it that umami richness. Serve it with your favorite dip-ables, like roasted veggies, really good whole-grain sourdough bread, and even sturdy greens like kale. This would make an equally amazing pasta sauce.

3 cups / 500g cooked white beans (such as butter beans, Great Northern, cannellini, etc.)

3 garlic cloves

½ cup / 30g nutritional yeast

¼ cup / 60ml cold-pressed olive oil

½ teaspoon fine sea salt

1½ teaspoons freshly squeezed lemon juice

2 tablespoons white miso (do not use dark miso)

1 teaspoon Dijon mustard

1 teaspoon raw honey or pure maple syrup

Cut-up raw vegetables, raw sturdy greens, and/or cubed whole-grain sourdough bread (gluten-free if desired) for dipping

1. Combine the beans, garlic, nutritional yeast, olive oil, salt, lemon juice, miso, mustard, and honey in a blender and blend on high speed, adding up to 1½ cups / 340ml water as necessary, until totally smooth and creamy. You are looking for a thick, cheeselike sauce. Season with more salt if necessary.

2. Pour the contents into a fondue pot or a saucepan that you can set on the table. Heat until just starting to bubble. Remove from the heat and serve immediately, with veggies, greens, and/or bread for dipping. Reheat as necessary. Store any leftovers, covered, in the fridge for 5 days.

MISO In general, lighter-colored miso pastes are milder and sweeter, and appropriate in salad dressings and light sauces, such as this recipe. Darker miso is typically used for braises, glazes, and gravies. The main ingredients in white miso are soybeans, rice, and barley, so it is high in both fiber and protein. Miso provides the body with a wide variety of phytonutrient antioxidants and anti-inflammatory substances. Because miso is fermented, it is probiotic, and therefore excellent for improving digestive health.

KANIWA Kaniwa is similar to quinoa and amaranth, a grain-like seed very high in protein and minerals. Because kaniwa is such a small seed, what we eat is mostly bran, which is very high in fiber and iron. The flavor of kaniwa is nutty and slightly sweet. It is delicious as a warm breakfast porridge and cold in a grain salad, too.

ROASTED CAULIFLOWER
WITH LEBANESE LENTILS AND KANIWA

SERVES 4 🟢 gf

Lebanese flavors are some of my favorites. Cumin, fennel, cinnamon, lemon, garlic—could it get any better? Folded through some tender kaniwa, lentils, and caramelized onions, apparently it can. I make this dish when I have leftover grains and legumes in the fridge, as it comes together quickly when these have been precooked. Although I've paired the kaniwa and lentils with golden roasted cauliflower, any vegetables would be delicious on the side, such as carrots, pumpkin, or beets.

1. Preheat the oven to 400°F / 200°C. Line a baking sheet with parchment paper.

2. Cut the cauliflower head into slices. Toss them with a little ghee and salt, and then arrange them in a single layer on the prepared baking sheet. Roast for 20 to 30 minutes, until the slices are browning on the edges.

3. Meanwhile, rinse and drain the kaniwa. Put it in a small saucepan, add just under 1 cup / 225ml of water and fine sea salt, and bring to a boil. Reduce the heat, and simmer until tender, about 15 minutes.

4. Rinse and drain the lentils. Put them in another small saucepan, add water to cover, and bring to a boil. Then reduce the heat and simmer until tender, about 20 minutes. About 5 minutes before the lentils are finished cooking, add a few pinches of flaky sea salt.

5. Heat a knob of ghee in a large saucepan over medium heat. Add the cumin seeds, cinnamon stick, fennel seeds, and black pepper. Cook until fragrant, 3 to 5 minutes. Add the sliced onions and cook, stirring often, until lightly caramelized, about 15 minutes. Add the cooked kaniwa and lentils, stir to combine, and reheat if necessary. Remove the cinnamon stick.

6. Whisk the olive oil, orange zest and juice, lemon juice, mint, parsley, fine sea salt, and honey together in a small bowl. Pour this over the lentils and kaniwa.

7. To serve, divide the kaniwa-lentil mixture, as well as the cauliflower slices, among four plates. Sprinkle with chopped mint and pink peppercorns. Serve warm.

1 head yellow cauliflower (white cauliflower is also fine)

Knob of ghee or coconut oil, melted

Flaky sea salt

½ cup / 125g kaniwa or quinoa

Fine sea salt

1 cup / 200g green lentils

2 teaspoons cumin seeds

1 cinnamon stick

1 teaspoon fennel seeds

½ teaspoon freshly cracked black pepper

3 small onions (about ¾ pound / 350g), sliced

2 tablespoons cold-pressed olive oil

Grated zest of 1 organic orange

2 tablespoons freshly squeezed orange juice

1½ tablespoon freshly squeezed lemon juice

⅓ cup / 7g chopped fresh mint leaves, plus more for garnish

⅓ cup / 7g chopped fresh parsley leaves

½ teaspoon fine sea salt

1 teaspoon raw honey

Pink peppercorns, for garnish

FOREST FLOOR FLATBREADS

MAKES 4 INDIVIDUAL PIZZAS

I am constantly inspired by the natural world—not just the food that the Earth provides, but the Earth itself: the seasons' textures, temperatures, and temperaments in a constant cycle of destruction and renewal. The autumn I find particularly stirring: I frequently walk in the woods near my home and watch the ground change from green grass to moist darkness, covered in mushrooms, vibrant leaves, and the occasional frost. I've tried to capture the colors and textures of the forest floor in this flatbread, and I really love the results. Not only does it taste amazing, but it looks almost scenic. There is more to enjoying the seasons than just cooking seasonally—taking our culinary cues from the outside world can be beautiful both to look at and to eat.

Knob of coconut oil or ghee

3 leeks, white parts only, sliced into rounds

Fine sea salt

1 medium sweet potato

1 chunk Pecorino Romano cheese (about 6 ounces / 175g)

4-Ingredient spelt pizza dough (page 95)

Kale-walnut pesto (recipe follows)

2 cups / 200g fresh chanterelle mushrooms

Freshly cracked black pepper

Cold-pressed olive oil, for garnish

Handful fresh oregano leaves, for garnish

1. Preheat the oven to 500°F / 260°C. If you have one, put a baking or pizza stone in the oven to warm up.

2. Melt the oil in a skillet over medium heat. Add the leeks and a few pinches of salt, and cook, stirring occasionally, until golden and caramelized, about 15 minutes. If the pan becomes dry, add a little water. Remove from the heat.

3. Using a mandoline, slice the sweet potato into very thin rounds. Slice the cheese into thin pieces.

4. To assemble a pizza, roll out one portion of the dough on a piece of parchment paper, forming a large round, about 10 inches / 25cm in diameter. Sprinkle it generously with salt, then spread about one-quarter of the kale pesto over the dough. Top with a quarter of the caramelized leeks, mushrooms, and sweet potato and cheese slices, and sprinkle with plenty of cracked black pepper.

5. Slide the flatbread onto a baking sheet or the preheated baking stone, and bake until the crust is golden, 5 to 7 minutes. Remove from the oven, drizzle with olive oil, sprinkle with oregano leaves, and serve. Repeat with the remaining dough and toppings.

KALE-WALNUT PESTO

MAKES ABOUT 1 CUP / 260G

Pulse the garlic in a food processor until minced. Add the kale, walnuts, lemon zest and juice, sea salt, maple syrup, and olive oil, and blend on high until chunky. Season with more salt if needed. Store in a glass container in the fridge for 4 to 5 days.

1 garlic clove

4 cups / 120g kale, tough stems removed, leaves chopped

1 cup / 140g raw walnuts, toasted if desired

Grated zest and juice of 1 small lemon

¼ teaspoon fine sea salt, plus more if needed

1 teaspoon pure maple syrup

2 tablespoons cold-pressed olive oil

10-SPICE CHOCOLATE CHILI

SERVES 6 Ⓥ ⓖⓕ

I will walk through fire to get to any kind of spicy chocolate concoction, and this chili is my new favorite way to warm up! Inspired by Mexican *mole negro*, a saucy combination of chiles, spices, herbs, ground nuts, tomatoes, and chocolate, I made a chili bursting with flavor and fire.

   This meal is a one-pot wonder that really satisfies and, with beans, corn, and veggies galore, it will give you some serious energy to burn. You can make this as spicy as you like, or keep it mild if you're cooking for children. The chocolate adds tons of depth and richness without the whole pot tasting like some crazy dessert. If your standard chili recipe needs resuscitation, put a fire under it and try this 10-spice version—it's guaranteed to heat things up!

3 medium onions

2 medium red bell peppers

2 medium sweet potatoes

2 ears fresh corn

4 garlic cloves

Knob of ghee or coconut oil

1 tablespoon cumin seeds

1 tablespoon coriander seeds

1 teaspoon fine sea salt

½ tablespoon ground cinnamon

½ tablespoon chipotle powder

½ teaspoon freshly cracked
   black pepper

¼ teaspoon ground cloves

⅛ teaspoon ground cayenne
   pepper, or to taste

Leaves from 6 or 7 large sprigs
   fresh thyme, or 1 tablespoon
   dried thyme leaves

Handful of fresh oregano leaves,
   or ½ tablespoon dried
   oregano

4 bay leaves

¼ cup / 30g unsweetened cocoa
   powder

1. Chop the onions, bell peppers, and sweet potatoes. Shuck the corn and slice the kernels off the cobs; you should have about 2 cups / 250g kernels. Mince the garlic.

2. Heat the ghee in a large pot over medium heat. When it has melted, add the cumin and coriander seeds. Cook for a couple of minutes, until fragrant. Add the chopped onions and the salt, and cook for 5 minutes, until softened. Add the garlic and cook for 1 minute.

3. Add the cinnamon, chipotle powder, black pepper, cloves, cayenne, bay leaves, thyme, oregano, and cocoa powder, and cook for a minute or two. If the pot gets dry, add some of the juice from the can of tomatoes.

4. Add the corn, bell peppers, sweet potatoes, beans, canned tomatoes with their juices, maple syrup, and 1½ cups / 340ml water. Cover and bring to a boil. Reduce the heat and simmer, stirring often, until the vegetables are tender, about 20 minutes. Stir in the lime juice and season to taste with more salt if desired.

5. Serve hot, garnished with the cilantro, pumpkin seeds, and lime wedges.

MAKING PERFECT PROTEIN It's true that beans are a very good source of plant-based protein, but unfortunately the protein in beans is not "complete." Beans are missing certain amino acids, the building blocks of protein, to make them equivalent to the proteins found in animal products. To remedy this, simply combine beans with certain foods to make up for the deficiency. Ancient cultures knew this instinctively, which is why we still embrace classic combinations such as rice and legumes, grains with leafy greens, peas and wheat, and in this case, corn and beans. Just by adding corn to the bean chili recipe here, you can be assured that you are getting the complete spectrum of essential amino acids required for proper protein synthesis, which is necessary for health and well-being.

1 (28-ounce / 800g) can whole tomatoes

2 cups / 350g cooked kidney beans or mixed beans (about one 15-ounce / 425g can)

1 tablespoon pure maple syrup

Freshly squeezed juice of ½ lime

Fresh cilantro leaves, for garnish

⅓ cup / 50g pumpkin seeds, lightly toasted, for garnish

1 lime, sliced into wedges, for garnish

ROASTED PUMPKIN WITH BLACK RICE AND TANGERINE TAHINI SAUCE

SERVES 4

There seems to be a common denominator in many of my favorite dishes, and that would quite simply be *sauce*. Why is it that dousing an already delicious meal with dressing is just the best thing ever? I derive so much joy out of it, you cannot even imagine. Or maybe you can, because you love sauce as much as I do. And what is this dish that's so worthy of liquid love? None other than roasted pumpkin on a bed of black rice with chile and garlic, drizzled with a tangerine tahini sauce. Enough said. (You can use any pumpkin you like for this recipe. Hokkaido pumpkins are popular here in Denmark, but I also like Delicata and Hubbard if available. Sweet potatoes or carrots would also be yummy.)

1½ cups / 250g black rice, soaked overnight if possible, rinsed, and drained

Fine sea salt

1 medium pumpkin about 2 pounds / 1kg, such as Hokkaido or Delicata

Knob of coconut oil or ghee, melted

2 garlic cloves, minced

Freshly cracked black pepper

½ cup / 10g chopped flat-leaf parsley

½ fresh chile, sliced (Serrano is a good choice)

Handful of raisins (optional)

Tangerine tahini sauce (recipe follows)

1. Put the rice and a few pinches of salt in a small saucepan, add 3 cups / 675ml water, and bring to a boil. Reduce the heat and simmer covered, until the water is absorbed, 25 to 50 minutes (depending on how long you soaked the rice). Remove from the heat.

2. While the rice is cooking, roast the pumpkin: Preheat the oven to 400°F / 200°C.

3. Wash the pumpkin skin well (if it's edible). Cut the pumpkin in half, then remove the seeds and slice the pumpkin into rounds or sections of approximately the same width. Put them in a single layer on a baking sheet, drizzle with melted oil, and sprinkle with the minced garlic and a few pinches of salt. Toss to coat. Roast the pumpkin until tender, about 30 minutes.

4. To serve, arrange the rice and pumpkin slices on each plate. Sprinkle with cracked black pepper, the chopped parsley, the chile, and the raisins if using. Drizzle with the tangerine tahini sauce. Serve extra sauce on the side.

BLACK RICE Black rice is an heirloom variety of rice cultivated in Asia. Sometimes referred to as "forbidden rice," it is typically sold unmilled, with the fiber-rich black husks still intact. It is this outer layer of bran that sets black rice apart from other types of unpolished rice, as the deep, dark pigments are evidence of its anthocyanins. The rice is rich in complex carbohydrates and good-quality digestible protein, yet low in fat.

TANGERINE TAHINI SAUCE

MAKES ABOUT 1½ CUPS / 350ML

Put the tahini, maple syrup, vinegar, tamari, tangerine zest and juice, ginger, and chile in a food processor or blender. Add ¼ cup / 56ml water, and blend on the highest setting until smooth. Season with salt if desired. Store any leftovers in a tightly sealed glass container in the fridge for up to 1 week.

½ cup / 125ml tahini

2 teaspoons pure maple syrup

2 teaspoons apple cider vinegar

1 tablespoon tamari

Grated zest of 1 organic tangerine

⅓ cup / 80ml freshly squeezed tangerine juice

¼ teaspoon ground ginger

½ fresh chile (Serrano is a good choice)

Flaky sea salt

PEAR APPLE BLACKBERRY CRUMBLE

SERVES 6 TO 8

The first summer I visited Copenhagen, I found the most abundant blackberry bramble on a path right beside my boyfriend's apartment. I am not joking when I say it was one of the things that tipped the scales in favor of my moving here—that is how much I love picking wild foods! I ate them by the handful fresh off the bush, and when my stomach couldn't take any more, I'd pick some more to put into this very crumble. In fact, I've made this dessert so many times over the years since then, I don't need to look at the ingredients list anymore. I suggest you make this part of your repertoire as well—it's so easy to throw together, and you can use any seasonal fruit, any time of the year.

1. Preheat the oven to 350°F / 180°C.

2. Peel the pears and apples if desired, chop them into bite-size chunks, and place them in a 9-inch/23cm baking dish. Add the blackberries and the lemon juice, and toss to coat.

3. Sprinkle the sugar, arrowroot, and 2 teaspoons of the cinnamon over the fruit, and toss to mix.

4. In a bowl, combine the rolled oats, maple syrup, walnuts, the remaining 1 teaspoon cinnamon, cardamom, flour, and salt. Cut in the cold coconut oil until the mixture is crumbly. Spread it over the fruit.

5. Bake the crumble for 25 to 30 minutes, until the fruit is bubbling and the top is golden brown. Let it cool slightly, and serve warm with yogurt or ice cream if desired.

BLACKBERRIES Blackberries don't travel or keep well, so picking them wild is your freshest and tastiest bet. They aren't hard to find, even if you live in a big city like Copenhagen! Blackberries contain good amounts of calcium, magnesium, and iron. They are also a source of cancer-preventing, anti-inflammatory ellagic acid.

2 large pears (about 1 pound / 400g)

2 large apples (about 1 pound / 400g)

3 cups / 350g blackberries

1 tablespoon freshly squeezed lemon juice

3 tablespoons coconut sugar

1 tablespoon arrowroot powder

3 teaspoons ground cinnamon

1¾ cups / 175g gluten-free rolled oats

⅓ cup / 80ml pure maple syrup

½ cup / 70g chopped raw walnuts

1 teaspoon ground cardamom

2 tablespoons whole-grain flour (such as gluten-free oat or rice)

¼ teaspoon fine sea salt

⅓ cup / 80g coconut oil or ghee, chilled

Raw cashew yogurt (page 116), or rawkin' funky monkey ice cream (page 153)

CHAI SPICE UPSIDE-DOWN PLUM CAKE

SERVES 10

When I think "upside-down cake," I get a very clear mental picture of that ubiquitous pineapple-and-maraschino-cherry number that everybody made in the 1980s: tooth-achingly sweet and anything but wholesome. My experiments with this classic dish certainly worked out. As if the moist chai-spiced cake itself was not delicious enough, a warm, oozy plum-caramel glaze really puts this one over the top. Not too sweet, and perfect with afternoon tea. It is particularly delicious served with something creamy and slightly sour, such as plain yogurt.

6 tablespoons / 90ml coconut oil or ghee, melted

¼ cup / 30g coconut sugar

4 to 5 small plums, pitted and thinly sliced

2½ cups / 300g whole spelt flour

2 teaspoons baking powder

1 teaspoon baking soda

1 teaspoon ground ginger

1½ teaspoons ground cardamom

1 teaspoon fennel seeds

¼ teaspoon ground cloves

2 teaspoons ground cinnamon

½ teaspoon ground star anise

½ teaspoon fine sea salt

¼ teaspoon freshly ground black pepper

1 cup / 240ml pure maple syrup or raw honey

¾ cup / 190ml milk of your choice (nut, seed, rice . . .)

2 teaspoons vanilla extract

1 teaspoon apple cider vinegar

1. Preheat the oven to 350°F / 180°C.

2. Coat the bottom of a 7-inch / 18cm springform cake pan with ½ tablespoon of the melted coconut oil, and sprinkle the coconut sugar evenly over it to cover the base. Neatly lay the plum slices in concentric rings on the bottom of the cake pan.

3. In a large mixing bowl, sift together the flour, baking powder, baking soda, and the ginger, cardamom, fennel seeds, cloves, cinnamon, star anise, salt, and pepper. Whisk to combine.

4. In a medium saucepan, melt the remaining 6 table-spoons coconut oil. Add the maple syrup, milk, and vanilla and whisk to combine. Pour the wet ingredients into the dry ingredients and whisk to remove any lumps. Add the vinegar and whisk quickly to incorporate.

5. Pour the batter into the cake pan, and put the pan on a rimmed baking sheet (to catch any liquid that may seep out while baking). Bake the cake until a toothpick inserted in the center comes out clean, 50 to 60 minutes.

6. When the cake has cooled, loosen the springform latch to open the pan. Invert a plate on the top of the cake, and swiftly invert the two together so that plums are now on the top. Serve.

PLUMS Plums are one of the few fruits that come in a wide variety of flavors and colors. They contain high amounts of two unique phytonutrients, neochlorogenic and chlorogenic acid. Research shows that these phenols are particularly effective in neutralizing free radicals and preventing oxidative cell damage.

WALNUT FIG BARS

These bars are a not-too-sweet treat that really highlights the delectable dried figs in the rich and gooey filling. The crust is made of oats and walnuts, all ground up with chia and applesauce to bind the ingredients together. Although these bars are in the sweets section, they would actually make a great breakfast on the go.

CRUST

1½ tablespoons chia seeds

2 cups / 280g raw walnuts

2 cups / 200g gluten-free rolled oats

¼ cup / 60g applesauce

2 tablespoons pure maple syrup

1 tablespoon coconut oil

1 teaspoon vanilla extract

¾ teaspoon fine sea salt

1 teaspoon baking powder

FILLING

2 cups / 300g dried figs

½ tablespoon ground cinnamon

½ teaspoon ground ginger

½ cup / 125g unsweetened applesauce

Grated zest of 1 organic lemon

¼ teaspoon fine sea salt

1. Make the crust: Combine the chia seeds with ¼ cup / 56ml water in a small bowl; set aside for 15 minutes to gel.

2. Put 1 cup / 140g of the walnuts on a baking sheet, put it in the oven, and set the oven temperature to 350°F / 180°C. Toast the walnuts while the oven is warming up (depending on how fast your oven heats up, this could take 5 to 15 minutes—just keep an eye on them to make sure they don't burn!). Remove from the oven and set the walnuts aside to cool. (Leave the oven on.)

3. In a food processor, process 1 cup / 100g of the oats on the highest setting until you have a rough flour. Add the toasted walnuts and blend again, until you have a sandy-textured meal. Add the chia gel, applesauce, maple syrup, coconut oil, and vanilla. Pulse until moist.

4. In a medium bowl, combine the remaining 1 cup / 100g rolled oats, ¾ teaspoon of the salt, and the baking powder. Add the processed oat mixture and fold to combine; you may need to use your hands.

5. Take about two-thirds of the crust mixture and press it firmly into an 8-inch- / 20cm-square baking pan. (It helps to wet your hands so that the dough doesn't stick.)

6. Make the filling: Wipe the food processor clean (no need to wash it). Roughly chop the figs and put them in the food processor, along with the cinnamon, ginger, applesauce, lemon zest, salt. Blend on the highest setting until the desired consistency is reached. (I leave mine a little chunky, but you can make it completely smooth.) Spread the filling evenly over the crust base.

7. Drop the remaining crust mixture in small chunks all over the filling, covering as much of it as possible. Roughly chop the remaining 1 cup / 140g walnuts and sprinkle them over the top; then lightly press the nuts into the crust. Bake for 25 to 30 minutes, until slightly golden on top. Let cool completely before cutting into bars. Store in the fridge, covered, for up to 5 days.

RAW CHOCOLATE NIGHT SKY

MAKES A GIANT CHOCOLATE BAR! 🅥 🅖🅕

At the risk of sounding overly sentimental, I take a lot of comfort in knowing that I am under the same sky as my family and friends back home in Canada. Sometimes seeing the moon appear and knowing that the people I hold dear can see the same one makes me feel less far away.

I came up with the idea for this chocolate while indulging in a homesick stargaze one night here in Denmark. As a black sky with a thousand twinkling lights stretched out above me, I found myself totally inspired and a little less sad, and I started dreaming about ways to capture the universe we all share in edible form. The "raw chocolate night sky" was born! A dark, rich chocolate bar studded with superfood stars, planets, and meteors. Sappy? Perhaps. But once you try this incredible treat, you'll forgive me.

1. In a double boiler (or in a heatproof glass bowl set over a pot of simmering water), melt the coconut oil and cacao butter together. Add the honey and whisk to combine. When the mixture is completely uniform, remove it from the heat and sift in the cacao powder, lucuma, maca, and sea salt. Taste for sweetness and saltiness, and adjust accordingly.

2. On a baking sheet lined with parchment paper, scatter half of the goji, cacao nibs, bee pollen, and hemp seeds. Wait until the liquid chocolate has cooled just slightly, so that it is a little thicker. Then pour the chocolate over the top, covering the superfoods in an even layer. Sprinkle the remaining half of the superfoods over the chocolate. Put the baking sheet in the fridge or freezer, and chill until the chocolate bar has firmed up completely, at least 1 hour in the fridge or 30 minutes in the freezer.

3. Break the cold chocolate bar into shards, or cut it into individual bars. Any leftovers can be wrapped in a plastic bag and stored in the freezer for 2 months.

½ cup / 120ml coconut oil

3 tablespoons cacao butter

⅓ cup / 75ml raw honey

¾ cup / 90g raw cacao powder

3 tablespoons lucuma powder

1 tablespoon maca powder

¼ teaspoon fine sea salt

¼ cup / 20g goji berries

¼ cup / 30g cacao nibs

1 tablespoon bee pollen

2 tablespoons hemp seeds

LUCUMA A starchy, caramel-tasting fruit sold as a powder, lucuma is deliciously sweet but low-glycemic, meaning that unlike sugar, it won't cause great spikes in blood glucose levels. It is considerably high in minerals, such as calcium, potassium, and magnesium. In this recipe it helps sweeten the chocolate and give it a nutrient boost.

NOTE When making raw chocolate, it is essential that all equipment be completely dry or the chocolate will seize up and you'll have to start over.

BANOFFEE PIE

SERVES 8

The first and only time I've ever been to London, I had one important goal: to eat a slice of banoffee pie. I'd fallen in love with the idea of bananas and caramel toffee all huddled together atop a crisp cookie crust . . . I mean, really? It was jaw-achingly sweet and certainly not made with whole food, but it gave me a great idea on how to make a version that was. My banoffee pie consists of a rolled oat and sunflower seed crust slathered with raw caramel toffee (delicious used as icing on cakes!) and cool coconut cream. Of course there are bananas, too. My version is totally pub-worthy, and I don't even think you'd need a couple of pints to agree with me.

½ cup / 70g sunflower seeds

2 cups / 200g gluten-free rolled oats

¼ teaspoon fine sea salt

¼ cup / 60ml coconut oil, chilled until very cold

2 tablespoons pure maple syrup

2 tablespoons ice water

2 (14-ounce / 400ml) cans full-fat coconut milk, chilled in the fridge overnight (so the cream separates and rises to the top)

Raw caramel toffee (recipe follows)

2 ripe bananas

A few squares of dark chocolate (optional)

1. Preheat the oven to 375°F / 190°C.

2. In a dry skillet over medium heat, toast the sunflower seeds until golden and fragrant, 3 to 5 minutes. Remove from the heat and put the sunflower seeds and the oats in a food processor. Let cool for a few minutes, and then blend on the highest setting until you have a rough, sandy flour. Add the salt, coconut oil, maple syrup, and ice water and pulse until everything is well incorporated and the dough holds together.

3. In a 7-inch / 18cm tart pan, press the dough down firmly over the bottom and up the sides. Prick the dough all over with a fork. Bake the crust for 20 to 30 minutes, until golden and crisp. Let the crust cool completely before filling it.

4. Without shaking the cans of coconut milk, open them up and scoop out the cream that has risen to the top. Put it in a bowl.

5. Spread a thick layer of raw caramel toffee over the cooled crust.

6. Slice the bananas and arrange half the slices in an even layer over the caramel layer. Spread the coconut cream on top, followed by another layer of bananas. Roughly chop or shave the chocolate if using, and sprinkle it over the top. Serve immediately.

RAW CARAMEL TOFFEE

MAKES 2 CUPS / 500ML

1. Soak the dates for at least 4 hours in water to cover. Drain the dates, reserving the soaking water.

2. Put the dates in a food processor, and add the nut butter, lemon juice, salt, and vanilla seeds. Blend on the highest setting until the caramel is smooth, adding the reserved soaking water, 1 tablespoon at a time, until the desired consistency is reached. You are looking for a thick, spreadable caramel for this recipe.

3. Store any leftovers in an airtight glass container in the fridge for up to 1 week.

1½ cups / 225g pitted Medjool dates

3 tablespoons nut or seed butter (almond, cashew, sesame tahini, sunflower . . .)

3 teaspoons freshly squeezed lemon juice

¼ teaspoon fine sea salt, or more to taste

½ vanilla bean, split lengthwise, seeds scraped out and reserved

WINTER

MORNINGS

CHAGA TEA

CHAGA HOT CHOCOLATE

CHUNKY BANANA BREAD GRANOLA

GINGER-ROSEMARY ROASTED GRAPEFRUIT WITH
    MACADAMIA NUT CREAM

CHIPOTLE SWEET POTATO AND TRUMPET MUSHROOM
    BREAKFAST TACOS

CRANBERRY CARROT LOAF

SMALL MEASURES

PICKLED FENNEL, GRAPEFRUIT, CABBAGE, AND AVOCADO SALAD

BEET PARTY WITH ORANGE AND PINE NUTS

ROASTED PARSNIPS WITH POMEGRANATE GLAZE AND ZA'ATAR

TRIPPY TIE-DYE SOUP

MAINS

FOUR CORNERS LENTIL SOUP

BUTTERNUT STACKS WITH KALE PESTO, KASHA, AND BUTTER BEANS

LEEK "SCALLOPS" AND CHANTERELLES ON BLACK RICE

GRAIN-FREE BLACK KALE SUSHI ROLLS WITH WHITE MISO
    GINGER SAUCE

SWEETS

CREAMY EGGNOG MILKSHAKE

PECAN CRANBERRY PIE

ROOIBOS-POACHED PEARS WITH RAW CHOCOLATE
    OLIVE OIL SAUCE

SALT 'N' PEPPER CHOCOLATE CHIP COOKIES

BLOOD ORANGE CHOCOLATE CAKE

CHAGA TEA

MAKES 1 QUART / 1 LITER

Although it has been used for hundreds of years, chaga mushroom is a new-to-me superfood. Harvested from the Canadian wilderness, it's no wonder these incredibly powerful fungi speak to me! Making a tea from these little 'shrooms is easy, and turning that tea into a luscious hot chocolate makes taking your medicine a truly indulgent experience. This is the perfect energizing breakfast drink, a wonderful afternoon pick-me-up, and a special after-dinner treat.

1. Put the chaga mushrooms in a saucepan, add 4 cups / 1 liter water, and bring to a simmer. Cook for 15 minutes until the water has taken on a dark-brown color.

2. Strain the tea through a fine-mesh sieve set over a large bowl, reserving both the liquid and the chaga.

3. Drink the tea immediately, or store it in a glass bottle in the fridge and consume within 1 week.

4. Put the used mushrooms in the freezer until you want to make more tea. You can rebrew chaga mushrooms three to six times before discarding them. You will know that the mushrooms are exhausted when you can no longer extract any brown pigment from them.

⅓ cup / 25g dried chaga mushrooms

CHAGA HOT CHOCOLATE

SERVES 1

Combine the chaga tea and milk in a small saucepan and warm over low-medium heat. When the mixture is warm, sift in the cacao powder and stir in the maple syrup. Enjoy warm.

CHAGA MUSHROOMS The benefits of chaga are simply astounding. The mushroom boasts one of the highest antioxidant ratings in the world. It contains over 200 phytonutrients and is currently being studied for cancer prevention and treatment. Chaga is rich in superoxide dismutase (SOD), an enzyme that strengthens the body's primary antioxidant systems. This helps to prevent aging, combat heart disease, and treat inflammation. Chaga is available in most health food stores, but it may be more convenient for most people to purchase it online.

½ cup / 125ml chaga tea

½ cup / 125ml milk of your choice (nut, hemp, rice . . .)

1 tablespoon raw cacao powder

1 tablespoon pure maple syrup or raw honey

CHUNKY BANANA BREAD GRANOLA

MAKES 9 CUPS / 18 SERVINGS

To say I'm obsessed with banana bread is an understatement—it's my kryptonite. Trying to figure out a way to eat it more often, I came up with a banana bread granola that tastes just like my favorite comfort food. I've made many a granola before, but this one beats them all! Not only does it have that rich banana flavor I dream about, but it's got a chunky quality to it that makes it perfect for snacking on right out of the jar. The secret to making chunky granola is using the bananas as a binding agent, fusing all those tasty ingredients together into crunchy, golden love clusters. Warning: This stuff is seriously addictive!

1. Preheat the oven to 350°F / 180°F. Line a baking sheet with parchment paper.

2. Melt the coconut oil in a small saucepan over low-medium heat. Pour the melted oil into a food processor or blender, add the bananas and maple syrup, and blend.

3. In a large bowl, combine the oats, buckwheat, coconut flakes, sunflower seeds, cinnamon, and salt. Roughly chop the walnuts and add them, too. Pour the liquid mixture over the dry mixture and fold to coat; this mix will be rather wet.

4. Spread the mixture out in an even layer on the prepared baking sheet, and press it firmly with the back of a spatula to ensure that the mixture is compact. Bake the granola for 15 to 20 minutes, until the mix is beginning to brown.

5. Remove the baking sheet from the oven, and use a spatula to flip the granola over in large sections. Return it to the oven and flip it every 3 to 4 minutes, making smaller chunks each time, until golden, for about another 15 minutes (for a total of 30 minutes or so). The granola should be dry and crispy. Set the granola aside at room temperature to cool. Do not stir the granola until it is completely cool, as this will help it set into chunks.

6. Store in an airtight container at room temperature for up to 1 month.

1/3 cup / 80ml coconut oil

3 very ripe bananas

1/2 cup / 120ml pure maple syrup

3 cups / 300g gluten-free rolled oats

1 cup / 185g buckwheat groats

1 1/2 cups / 65g large, unsweetened coconut flakes

1/2 cup / 70g sunflower seeds

2 teaspoons ground cinnamon

1/2 teaspoon fine sea salt

1 cup / 140g whole raw walnuts

GINGER-ROSEMARY ROASTED GRAPEFRUIT WITH MACADAMIA NUT CREAM

SERVES 4

The delicious smell of this simple breakfast will rouse even the sleepiest person out of bed. Although it is a surprising combination of flavors, rosemary and ginger work very well together in a sophisticated twist on the classic broiled grapefruit. The macadamia nut cream is rich and luscious and can be used in place of whipped cream at any time. This delicious yet simple breakfast could easily double as dessert. (The macadamia nut cream really needs a high-speed blender, so if you do not have one, substitute plain yogurt or sour cream.)

4 large grapefruit

3 tablespoons coconut sugar

2 teaspoons finely minced fresh rosemary, plus more for garnish if desired

½ teaspoon ground ginger

Macadamia nut cream (recipe follows)

1. Preheat the oven to Broil. Line a baking sheet with parchment paper.

2. Cut each grapefruit in half; you may need to cut a small piece off the bottom of each half so they sit up straight. Using a small knife, cut all the way around each section, between the fruit and the membranes, so the fruit can be easily removed once roasted.

3. Combine the coconut sugar, minced rosemary, and ginger in a small bowl. Sprinkle about ½ tablespoon of this mixture over each grapefruit half. Put the grapefruit, cut side up, on the prepared baking sheet and broil for about 10 minutes, until fragrant. Remove from the oven and set aside to cool for a few minutes.

4. To serve, put 2 grapefruit halves on each plate, spoon the macadamia nut cream over the top, and garnish with additional rosemary if desired. Enjoy.

MACADAMIA NUT CREAM

MAKES ABOUT 1 CUP / 250ML

1 cup / 140g raw macadamia nuts (cashews work as well)

1 vanilla bean, split lengthwise, seeds scraped out and reserved

3 tablespoons pure maple syrup

2 pinches fine sea salt

1. Soak the macadamia nuts overnight, or for at least 4 hours. Drain and rinse well.

2. Put the nuts, vanilla seeds, maple syrup, salt, and ½ cup / 112ml water in a high-speed blender and blend until smooth. Store any leftovers in an airtight glass container in the fridge for up to 4 days.

CHIPOTLE SWEET POTATO AND TRUMPET MUSHROOM BREAKFAST TACOS

SERVES 4

When I go out to a restaurant for breakfast, my eyes are like heat-seeking missiles searching for the words *breakfast tacos*. Breakfast tacos are most definitely a North American phenomenon, so here in Copenhagen, I am pretty much forced to make my own. These little beauties feature my favorite tuber, the sweet potato, all spiced up with smoky chipotle. I'm hoping my version of breakfast tacos will change the collective consciousness in this city and I'll see something similar on a menu here soon. Until then, I'll just be thankful I don't need to change out of my pajamas to eat them. (There's no need to limit yourself to making this for breakfast, either—this meal would make a delicious lunch or dinner.)

Freshly squeezed juice of 1 lime

2 teaspoons cold-pressed olive oil, plus more for garnish if desired

1 teaspoon raw honey or pure maple syrup

2 cups / 175g shredded cabbage

Handful fresh cilantro, chopped

Fine sea salt

2 knobs of ghee or coconut oil

1 small red onion, sliced

3 garlic cloves, minced

2 teaspoons ground cumin

½ teaspoon chipotle powder or hot smoked paprika

Pinch of cayenne pepper, or more to taste

2 large sweet potatoes (about 1 pound / 500g), cubed (leave the skin on if organic)

2 tablespoons tomato paste

1 cup / 225 ml water or vegetable broth

2 handfuls (5 ounces / 150g) trumpet mushrooms (or any mushroom you like), sliced

Freshly ground black pepper

1. In a large bowl, whisk together the lime juice, olive oil, and honey. Add the shredded cabbage, cilantro, and sea salt to taste. Toss well.

2. Heat a knob of ghee in a large skillet. Add the onion and a couple pinches of salt. Cook until the onion has softened, about 5 minutes. Add the garlic, cumin, chipotle, and cayenne, and cook for another minute or so. Add the sweet potatoes, tomato paste, and water or broth. Cook, covered, until the sweet potatoes have softened, about 10 minutes. Remove from the heat, set the mixture aside, and wipe out the pan. Return the pan to the heat.

3. Heat another knob of ghee in the hot pan. Add the mushrooms, making sure there is enough space between them to cook. Do not stir them for about 5 minutes—this will allow them brown a little on one side. Then flip them over and cook for another 3 to 4 minutes, until golden. Season with salt and pepper. If you're using them, add the beans to the pan and heat until warmed through.

4. In a dry skillet over medium-high heat, warm each of the tortillas, then wrap to keep hot until serving. To serve, put a helping of the sweet potatoes on each tortilla, followed by a few slices of mushrooms. Garnish with the cabbage slaw. Serve with hot sauce alongside.

1½ cups / 250g cooked beans (approx. 1 14-ounce can) of your choice (optional)

4 large or 8 small sprouted corn tortillas (Ezekiel brand is good)

Your favorite hot sauce, for serving

SWEET POTATOES To skin or not to skin? If you can find organic sweet potatoes, most definitely leave the skin on! It's the most nutrient-dense part of the tuber, including some nutrients not found in the flesh. When you eat the skin, you are getting more fiber and beta-carotene, iron, vitamin E, and folate. Remember that you need some fat with your sweet potato to be able to absorb both beta-carotene and vitamin E, so don't skimp on the ghee or olive oil!

CRANBERRY CARROT LOAF

MAKES 1 LOAF

This bread is pretty much an excuse to eat carrot cake for breakfast! Super-moist and tender, loaded with tart cranberries—you won't believe that it's good for you. Take a slice with you on the way to work, and pack an extra one in your lunch box for good measure. Your four-o'clock tummy rumbles will thank you.

1. In a small bowl, combine the chia seeds and milk. Stir, and let sit at room temperature for at least 15 minutes to gel.

2. Meanwhile, preheat the oven to 350°F / 180°C. Lightly grease a standard loaf pan with coconut oil.

3. Melt the coconut oil in a small saucepan over medium heat, and then stir in the orange zest and vanilla seeds. Remove from the heat.

4. Put the carrots in a medium bowl. Add the maple syrup, the milk-chia gel, and the coconut oil mixture.

5. In a large bowl, whisk together the spelt flour, oats, cinnamon, ginger, cloves, baking powder, baking soda, and salt. Pour the wet ingredients over the dry ingredients, and stir until just combined. Fold in the cranberries.

6. Pour the mixture into the prepared loaf pan. Bake for 45 minutes or until a toothpick inserted in the center comes out clean. Let the cake cool in the pan for 10 minutes, and then transfer the loaf to a wire rack to cool completely. The bread will keep wrapped at room temperature for 5 days. Store in the freezer for up to 2 months.

CRANBERRIES Because of their potent nutrition and unique health-promoting properties, cranberry extracts are readily available in supplement form, but studies show that eating the berries whole (surprise, surprise) does a better job at protecting our liver and cardiovascular system. Again, we must remember that breaking foods down into their individual constituents doesn't always make sense—food is whole for a reason. Cranberries are an excellent example of this, so get those whole berries into a carrot loaf pronto!

1 tablespoon chia seeds

½ cup / 125ml milk of your choice (nut, seed, rice . . .)

¼ cup / 60ml coconut oil, plus extra for oiling the pan

2 teaspoons grated organic orange zest

½ vanilla bean, split lengthwise, seeds scraped out and reserved, or 1 teaspoon vanilla extract

1½ loosely packed cups / 140g grated carrots (about 2 medium carrots)

½ cup / 125ml pure maple syrup

1½ cups / 180g whole spelt flour

½ cup / 50g rolled oats

1 tablespoon ground cinnamon

1 teaspoon ground ginger

½ teaspoon ground cloves

2 teaspoons baking powder

½ teaspoon baking soda

¼ teaspoon fine sea salt

¾ cup / 80g cranberries, fresh or frozen

PICKLED FENNEL, GRAPEFRUIT, CABBAGE, AND AVOCADO SALAD

SERVES 4

I don't eat a lot of raw food in the wintertime, but this salad is a refreshing exception. The pickled fennel is bursting with citrus and ginger flavors, waking up a sleepy palate. You can use it in a number of dishes, both cooked and raw, or just on the side of a warming stew to cut through the richness. There is a great balance here between the briny fennel, crisp cabbage, creamy avocado, and tangy grapefruit, spiced up with the warmth of pink peppercorns. This salad is incredibly helpful for the digestion because it is totally raw and loaded with enzymes. Although it is a wonderful start to a meal, I like to enjoy this cleansing salad at the end.

PICKLED FENNEL

1 large fennel bulb

1 cup / 225 ml apple cider vinegar

1 tablespoon pure maple syrup or raw honey

½ tablespoon fine sea salt

1 small organic orange

5 whole star anise

1 tablespoon minced fresh ginger

SALAD

¼ head purple cabbage

2 tablespoons cold-pressed olive oil

A couple pinches of flaky sea salt

2 large grapefruits

1 large ripe avocado

Fresh parsley leaves, for garnish

2 teaspoons crushed pink peppercorns

1. Pickle the fennel: Using a mandoline slicer, slice the fennel into very thin strips.

2. In a measuring cup, combine the vinegar, maple syrup, and fine sea salt with 1 cup / 225ml water. Stir well.

3. Slice the orange (unpeeled) into thin rounds. Put a couple slices at the bottom of a quart/liter jar and add a handful of fennel, 1 star anise, and a little of the ginger. Continue to stack the oranges, fennel, star anise, and ginger until you've used up all the ingredients or have reached the top of the jar. Pour the brine into the jar, completely covering the contents; discard any excess brine. Put an airtight lid on the jar, and store it in the fridge for 24 hours. After that, the pickled fennel can be enjoyed for up to 3 weeks.

4. Make the salad: Using a mandoline slicer, shred the cabbage very thin and put it in a bowl. Add a tablespoon or so of the pickled fennel juice, plus a tablespoon of olive oil and some flaky sea salt. Toss to combine.

5. Slice the rind off the grapefruits and cut the fruit into wedges. Pit the avocado and slice it into sections.

6. Divide the cabbage, grapefruit, avocado, and pickled fennel among four plates. Drizzle with the remaining olive oil and sprinkle with parsley and crushed pink peppercorns. Enjoy.

PURPLE CABBAGE Purple cabbage has got to be one of the healthiest foods that you are probably not eating. It's loaded with detoxifying minerals such as sulfur and choline and boasts significantly more protective phytonutrients than green cabbage, due to its deep pigmentation. I find the very best way to enjoy cabbage is to thinly shred it on a mandoline, making the cabbage so delicate and really pleasurable to eat. This process takes seconds (way faster than with a knife) and adds amazing crunch and color to many meals in the blink of an eye.

BEET PARTY WITH ORANGE AND PINE NUTS

I am always surprised to discover how few people know that beets can be eaten raw. They are truly delicious this way! The beet party includes both raw and roasted beets, for the ultimate mix of textures and flavors. Roasted beets are deeply sweet and velvety, while raw beets are earthy and very crunchy. You will be amazed that they are the same vegetable. This salad is a total flavor fest, celebrating beets, oranges, fresh parsley, and pine nuts. Black lentils add texture and tons of protein and fiber. It is altogether fresh and alive—the perfect party to attend this winter.

½ cup / 100g black lentils, soaked (overnight if possible)

Fine sea salt

6 mixed beets (2 pounds / 1kg; red, golden, white, Chioggia . . .)

¼ cup / 60 ml cold-pressed olive oil

3 tablespoons apple cider vinegar

2 teaspoons raw honey or pure maple syrup

Grated zest of 2 organic oranges

½ cup / 10g chopped flat-leaf parsley

¼ cup / 35g raw pine nuts, lightly toasted

Freshly cracked black pepper

1. Preheat the oven to 400°F / 200°C.

2. Drain and rinse the lentils, put them in a saucepan, and cover with water. Bring to a boil, reduce the heat, and simmer until tender but not mushy, 10 to 20 minutes, depending on the soaking time. When the lentils are almost cooked, add ¾ teaspoon salt and continue to simmer until tender. Drain, and rinse under cold water to halt the cooking. Put the lentils in a large bowl.

3. Wrap 4 beets in aluminum foil and put them on a baking sheet. Roast the beets until they are cooked through, 35 to 50 minutes, depending on their size. Remove from the oven, let sit in their foil for about 15 minutes, and when they are cool enough to handle, unwrap the foil and slip the skins off. Chop the beets into bite-size pieces and add them to the lentils.

4. Peel the remaining 2 beets. Using a mandoline or a sharp knife, slice the beets into thin rounds; then slice the rounds crosswise to make matchsticks. Add the raw beets to the lentils and roasted beets.

5. Whisk the olive oil, vinegar, honey, and a pinch of salt together in a small bowl, and pour this dressing over the salad. Add the orange zest, chopped parsley, and pine nuts, and season with salt and pepper. Enjoy.

PINE NUTS Pine nuts are high in monounsaturated and polyunsaturated fatty acids. They contain good amounts of protein, fiber, calcium, iron, and magnesium. Because they tend to spoil very quickly, always look for them in the refrigerated section of the grocery store to ensure that they are fresh.

ROASTED PARSNIPS WITH POMEGRANATE GLAZE AND ZA'ATAR

SERVES 4

Za'atar is like fairy dust: sprinkle a little on a rather ho-hum meal and suddenly you've got something that sparkles! I always have some on hand to dress up roasted veggies, sandwiches, and salads . . . and it also comes in handy when you've got guests coming over and all you have is a bunch of carrots. *Poof!* Now you have magical fairy-dust fancy carrots.

In this recipe, I use parsnips, which are in the same family as carrots but mysteriously less popular. They are sweet and creamy with an earthy side that I really dig with sour flavors, such as pomegranate molasses and sumac. Combined with sesame seeds, garlic, mint, and pomegranate seeds, this dish is anything but ho-hum.

1. Preheat the oven to 400°F / 200°C.

2. Whisk the pomegranate molasses, olive oil, and flaky salt together in a small bowl. Season to taste.

3. Peel the parsnips and cut them into sticks about the size of large French fries. In a medium bowl, toss the sticks with a little melted ghee, the minced garlic, and flaky sea salt and cracked black pepper. Spread the parsnips out on a large baking sheet and roast for 25 to 35 minutes, until tender.

4. Put the roasted parsnips on a platter and drizzle with the pomegranate glaze, a generous sprinkling of za'atar, pomegranate seeds, and the chopped mint.

SUMAC The condiment za'atar is based on is sumac (*Rhus coriaria*), a spice that comes from the berries of a wild bush that grows in the Mediterranean region. It is an essential ingredient in Arab cooking for delivering sourness and astringency. When the berry is dried, it is ground to a powder and has a tart lemony taste. Aside from being a tasty treat, sumac berries' deep pigments are evidence of the high concentration of the compound anthocyanins, which help to decrease the risk of heart disease and cancer. You can purchase the deep reddish-brown ground sumac at most ethnic groceries and spice shops.

2 tablespoons pomegranate molasses (or use 2 tablespoons pure maple syrup plus 1 teaspoon freshly squeezed lemon juice)

2 tablespoons olive oil

2 pinches flaky sea salt

8 medium parsnips (2 pounds / 1kg; you can also use parsley root or celeriac)

Knob of ghee or coconut oil, melted

2 garlic cloves, minced

Flaky sea salt and freshly cracked black pepper

Seeds from 1 small pomegranate (about ½ cup / 90g)

Za'atar (page 44), for garnish

Handful fresh mint leaves, roughly chopped

TRIPPY TIE-DYE SOUP

SERVES 6 TO 8

Trip out! This is one mind-bending bowl of soup—two tastes twirled together into psychedelic deliciousness. You may think I'm high to suggest making two different soups for one meal, but trust me, I'm stone-cold sober and dead serious. The smoky beet soup is a vibrant magenta, delicious and visually stunning when swirled around the rich and creamy white bean soup. These two tastes together are so complementary—it's peace, love, and harmony in a bowl. The easiest way to make this soup is to begin by preparing all the ingredients, then cooking the two soups side by side on the stove.

4 medium onions (about 1 pound / 450g)

3 large leeks, white and pale-green parts only, sliced

2 tablespoons coconut oil or ghee

Fine sea salt

7 garlic cloves

1 teaspoon smoked paprika

3 medium beets (about 1½ pounds / 675g), peeled and roughly chopped

4½ cups / 1.1 liters vegetable broth

2 cups / 330g cooked white beans (about one 15-ounce / 350g can)

2 tablespoons cold-pressed olive oil

Freshly cracked black pepper

1 teaspoon freshly squeezed lemon juice

Chopped fresh flat-leaf parsley or chives, for garnish (optional)

1. Chop the onions and leeks, and divide them between two separate pots. Divide the coconut oil between the two pots. Heat both pots over medium-high heat and stir to coat the vegetables with the oil. Season with sea salt. Let cook for 5 to 10 minutes, until softened.

2. Mince 3 garlic cloves. Add the minced garlic and the paprika to one of the pots, and cook for another minute. Then add the beets and 2 cups / 450ml of the broth, and bring to a boil. Reduce the heat and simmer until the beets are fork-tender, 15 to 20 minutes.

3. Meanwhile, mince the remaining 4 garlic cloves. Add that minced garlic to the second pot of onions and leeks and cook for a couple minutes. Add the beans, the remaining 2½ cups / 560ml broth. Bring to a boil, reduce the heat, and simmer until the beet soup is ready.

4. Ladle the bean soup into a blender. Add 1 tablespoon of the olive oil and blend on high speed until completely smooth. Season with salt and pepper. Pour the soup back into the pot.

5. Without cleaning the blender, ladle the beet soup into it. Add the lemon juice and the remaining 1 tablespoon olive oil, and blend on high speed until completely smooth. Season with salt and pepper. Pour the soup back into the pot.

6. To serve, ladle one soup into each bowl, followed by the other soup on the other side. Using a toothpick, swirl the soups together into a tie-dye pattern. Have fun with it! Garnish with chopped parsley. Serve hot.

FOUR CORNERS LENTIL SOUP

SERVES 4

My favorite recipe that I've ever posted on the blog is my Four Corners lentil soup, and it remains the most frequently cooked dish in my kitchen. It is so fast and simple to make, really inexpensive, and uses ingredients that are all found in the pantry. It freezes well, too, so I often make a double batch and store some away for when I need a wholesome meal in a hurry. And why the name "Four Corners"? Besides being my favorite soup, it is also much loved by many people I know all around the world. From the busy streets of Singapore to the remote wilderness of northern Ontario, from the scorched deserts in the American Southwest to the rainy shores of Denmark, this soup really has traveled the four corners of the Earth! Highly nutritious and packed with flavor, this lentil soup is a crowd-pleaser that will warm the heart of anyone you serve it to.

1. Heat the oil in a medium pot, add the onions, garlic, and ginger, and sauté for 5 minutes, until soft. Add a pinch of salt, the cumin, and the cayenne, and stir for another minute or so, until fragrant.

2. Add the tomatoes, 3 slices of lemon, and the lentils. Then add the vegetable broth and stir well. Cover the pot and bring the mixture to a boil. Reduce the heat and simmer for about 30 minutes, until the lentils are soft. Add a squirt of maple syrup to balance the flavor, if desired.

3. Serve hot, garnished with the cilantro, spring onions, or parsley, and topped with a slice of lemon.

RED LENTILS Red lentils have a velvety texture and a delicate flavor—perfect for purees and soups because they tend to fall apart when cooked. I often add blended red lentils to soups or stews to make them creamy without the cream! They are low in calories, virtually fat-free, but very filling because of their high fiber content. In addition to providing the body with slow-burning complex carbohydrates, lentils can increase your energy by replenishing your iron stores. This is a particularly good feature for women, who are more at risk for iron deficiency—especially because, unlike red meat, another source of iron, lentils are not rich in fat and calories.

1 tablespoon coconut oil or ghee

2 large onions or leeks, white and pale-green parts only, chopped

5 garlic cloves, minced

1 tablespoon minced fresh ginger

Fine sea salt

1 tablespoon ground cumin

¼ teaspoon cayenne pepper, or more to taste

1 (15-ounce / 400g) can whole tomatoes, or 5 large fresh tomatoes chopped

1 small organic lemon, sliced

1 cup / 200g red lentils, picked over and rinsed very well (soaked, if possible)

4 cups / 1 liter vegetable broth

Pure maple syrup or raw honey (optional)

Fresh cilantro leaves, sliced spring onions, or flat-leaf parsley leaves, for garnish

BUTTERNUT STACKS WITH KALE PESTO, KASHA, AND BUTTER BEANS

SERVES 3 TO 4 gf

This dish came to me when I was sick of making salads over and over again. I realized that just by changing the way I present food on a plate, I could turn an ordinary dish into something special and fit to impress my best guests.

The kasha and butter bean salad is lovely on its own, perhaps with the goat cheese thrown in if you eat dairy. I should tell you that kasha is an acquired taste for many people. If you are making this dish for the first time, try the kasha before adding in all the other ingredients, just to be sure you like it. If not, you can use any other grain, such as brown rice, quinoa, or millet, in its place.

4 cups / 120g kale, tough ribs removed, leaves roughly chopped

1 cup / 140g raw walnuts

1 garlic clove

Grated zest and juice of 1 organic lemon

Fine sea salt

1 teaspoon pure maple syrup

2 to 3 tablespoons cold-pressed olive oil, plus more for garnish

Neck of 1 butternut squash (2 pounds / 1kg; purchase one with the longest neck you can find)

Knob of coconut oil or ghee

Freshly cracked black pepper

1 cup / 200g kasha (toasted buckwheat)

1½ cups / 250g cooked butter beans (any white bean will do)

4½ ounces / 125g soft goat cheese

1. Put the chopped kale in a food processor, and add the walnuts, garlic, lemon zest and juice, ¼ teaspoon sea salt, maple syrup, and 2 tablespoons olive oil. Blend on the highest setting until the desired consistency. This pesto is quite dry, so add more olive oil if desired. (The pesto will keep in an airtight glass container in the fridge for 4 to 5 days.)

2. Preheat the oven to 400°F / 200°C. Line a baking sheet with parchment paper.

3. Peel the squash and slice it into rounds approximately ¾ inch / 2cm thick; aim to have 12 to 16 slices. Lightly coat the slices with oil, sprinkle with salt and pepper, and put them on the prepared baking sheet. Bake for 25 to 30 minutes, until tender.

4. Meanwhile, rinse the kasha well, then put it in a saucepan and add ½ teaspoon salt and 2 cups / 450ml water. Bring to a boil, reduce the heat, and simmer, covered, for 15 to 20 minutes, until the kasha is tender and the water has been absorbed.

5. In a large bowl, combine the cooked kasha, butter beans, and enough kale pesto to coat everything well. Toss to combine. Season with salt and pepper.

6. To assemble, put 1 round of butternut squash on a plate. Spread the round with goat's cheese, and top it with about ¼ cup / 50g of the kasha mixture. Top with another round of butternut squash, and repeat on the other plates. Enjoy immediately.

KASHA Raw buckwheat is a pale-greenish color whereas kasha is distinctly brown because it has been roasted. Kasha has a nutty flavor and chewy texture, making it a perfect choice for both savory and sweet dishes. Kasha and buckwheat are not actually true grains, but rather the fruit seed of a plant in the rhubarb family. Kasha is high in protein, especially the amino acids lysine and arginine. Unlike most grains, buckwheat is low on the glycemic scale and can actually help stabilize blood sugar.

LEEKS Leeks belong to the allium family of vegetables, along with garlic and onions. As a result, they contain many of the same beneficial compounds found in those well-researched, health-promoting vegetables. One very important nutrient concentrated in leeks is the B vitamin folate. The highest concentration of folate is in a leek's white bulb portion (about 50% more than in the rest of the stalk), but there is still enough folate in the green parts to also be considered beneficial.

LEEK "SCALLOPS" AND CHANTERELLES ON BLACK RICE

SERVES 4

This is the kind of meal you'll want to curl up with on a snowy winter night. It's hearty, comforting, and just plain delicious. I cannot remember where I heard of someone using the whites of leeks in place of scallops, but I thought it was so brilliant I had to try it, too. Cooking them with a little broth in the pan to steam and flavor them cuts back on fat but seriously enhances the taste. The savory-sweet leeks pair very well with the rich chanterelle mushrooms. The black rice completes the plate with its complex creaminess and beautiful hue.

1. In a small saucepan set over medium heat, combine the rice, 2 pinches of salt, and 3 cups / 675ml water. Bring to a boil, reduce the heat, cover the pan, and simmer until the water has been absorbed, about 45 minutes. Remove from the heat.

2. Slice the white part of the leeks into rounds about the width of a scallop (about 1 inch / 2.5cm).

3. In a large skillet, over medium heat, melt a knob of ghee. Add the garlic and fry just until golden, about 2 minutes. Add the mushrooms and a pinch of salt, and toss to coat. Cook without stirring for about 5 minutes (this will allow the mushrooms to brown on one side). Then flip them over and fry until golden on the other side. Remove from the pan, cover, and keep warm.

4. Without cleaning the pan, pour in the vegetable broth and bring it to a simmer. Add the leek rounds to the pan, cover, and cook, flipping them once, for 5 to 6 minutes, until tender.

5. To serve, put a quarter of the black rice on each plate. Top with the mushrooms and the leek rounds. Drizzle with olive oil, sprinkle with cracked black pepper, and add a sprinkling of chives, if using. Serve hot.

1½ cups / 320g black rice, soaked if possible

Fine sea salt

3 large leeks, as fat as you can find, with long white stalks

2 knobs of ghee or coconut oil (preferably ghee)

5 garlic cloves, sliced

14 ounces / 400g chanterelle mushrooms, sliced in half if large

½ cup / 112ml vegetable broth

Cold-pressed olive oil, for drizzling

Freshly cracked black pepper

Chopped fresh chives, for garnish (optional)

GRAIN-FREE BLACK KALE SUSHI ROLLS WITH WHITE MISO GINGER SAUCE

MAKES 4 TO 5 ROLLS, 25 TO 30 PIECES

As much as I love sushi, my favorite part is undoubtedly what's inside the rolls—the white rice I could live without. So I cut out the rice altogether and created an all-vegetable sushi roll that is just as satisfying but more nutritious. Minced parsley root and sunflower seeds take the place of the grain here; it holds together just like sticky rice, and even looks the part! Rolled around some of my favorite root veggies, this totally raw meal will have you feeling super-vibrant in the dark depths of winter. The white miso ginger sauce is completely divine and a beautiful complement to the sushi. It's warming, bright, and spicy—delicious on noodles, roasted vegetables, and salads, too.

1. Make the "rice": Combine the sunflower seeds, 1½ tablespoons salt, and 2 cups / 450ml of water in a small bowl, and soak for at least 4 hours, or overnight. Drain and rinse well.

2. Put the sunflower seeds in a food processor and pulse to finely chop—do not overprocess or you'll end up with sunflower butter! Transfer the sunflower seeds to a large bowl. Do not clean the food processor.

3. Peel and roughly chop the parsley root. Put it in the food processor, along with the lemon juice and the remaining ½ teaspoon salt. Pulse to mince the root into "grains" about the size of rice. Add it to the bowl of sunflower seeds and fold to combine. Season with more salt if desired.

4. Put a sushi mat (or a piece of plastic wrap) on a clean cutting board with the slats running horizontally. Put a sheet of nori, shiny side down, on the mat, ¾ inch / 2cm from the edge closest to you. Using damp hands, spread a thin layer of the "rice" evenly over the nori sheet, leaving a 1¼-inch- / 3cm-wide border along the edge farthest from you. Arrange about one-fifth of the kale, beet, carrot, scallions, and avocado strips horizontally across the center of the rice, and then sprinkle with sesame seeds.

1 cup / 140g sunflower seeds

1½ tablespoons plus ½ teaspoon fine sea salt, more if desired

4 parsley roots (1 pound / 500g; parsnips or cauliflower could also work)

1 tablespoon freshly squeezed lemon juice

4 or 5 sheets nori

5 to 10 leaves black kale or other dark leafy green, tough ribs removed, leaves cut into thin strips

1 small beet cut into long, thin sticks

2 medium carrots cut into long, thin sticks

3 scallions, white and green parts cut into long, thin sticks

1 ripe avocado, pitted and sliced into long, thin strips

Black or white sesame seeds, lightly toasted

White miso ginger sauce (page 228)

(RECIPE CONTINUES)

- Cut all the vegetables to a consistent width so you don't create a bulge in the roll—this can encourage the nori to split.

- Be careful not to overstuff the roll. It is not a burrito.

- Select a maximum of four or five fillings per roll. You want to allow each ingredient to shine—with too many elements, the flavors of the individual fillings become muddled.

- Moisten your hands as you assemble the rolls, especially when spreading rice over the nori. Keep a small bowl of lukewarm water next to where you are working so that you can continually dip your hands as needed. You can also use this water to moisten the bare far edge of the nori sheet to create a seal so the roll stays closed.

- Use a very sharp knife. This is where ceramic knives really come in handy! Of course a sharp metal knife is totally fine—just make sure it has a razor edge, or you'll end up with a big, smashed-up mess.

- It is important to wipe the blade of the knife clean with a damp cloth after every single slice of the roll.

5. Use your thumbs and forefingers to pick up the edge of the mat closest to you. Use your other fingers to hold the filling while you roll the mat over to enclose it. Gently pull the mat as you go to create a firm roll.

6. Continue rolling until all the "rice" is covered with the nori and you have a neat roll. Shape your hands around the mat to gently tighten the roll. Use a wet sharp knife to cut the roll into 5 or 6 pieces.

7. Repeat the process, using up all the ingredients. Arrange the sushi on a serving platter and serve with the white miso ginger sauce.

NORI Nori is probably the most widely eaten and recognizable sea vegetable in North America because of our love affair with sushi. It has a very mild, nutty, salty-sweet thing going on, so it is a versatile ocean vegetable that doesn't overpower the flavor of soups, salads, grains, or even popcorn. Nori has the highest protein content of the sea vegetable family, a whopping 28% (that's even more than sunflower seeds or lentils!). It contains very high amounts of calcium, iron, manganese, zinc, and copper. Compared to other seaweeds, it also tops the list when it comes to vitamins B_1, B_2, B_3, B_6, and B_{12}, as well as A, C, and E.

WHITE MISO GINGER SAUCE

MAKES ABOUT ½ CUP / 125 ML

¼ cup / 60ml white miso

½ tablespoon brown rice vinegar

2 tablespoons cold-pressed sesame oil or olive oil

1 tablespoon minced fresh ginger

½ teaspoon pure maple syrup

Combine the miso, vinegar, oil, ginger, and maple syrup in a small bowl. Whisk to blend. Store leftovers in an airtight container in the fridge for up to 1 week.

CREAMY EGGNOG MILKSHAKE

SERVES 1 Ⓥ ⓖⓕ ☾

I always know that Christmas is right around the corner when eggnog suddenly appears in my parents' fridge. My father just loves the stuff, but although the smell really appeals to me, the idea of drinking raw yolks kind of turns me off. Once I realized that it was the sweetness and the scent of freshly grated nutmeg that charmed me, I set out to make a raw vegan version that would satisfy even my dad's discriminating palate. It's super-rich, thick, and creamy—an amazing breakfast, but decadent enough for dessert. The sesame seeds are an unusual addition to a milkshake, but give them a try! They add tons of protein, fiber, healthy fats, and calcium and help make this smoothie a veritable meal.

1. Put the sesame seeds, figs, and salt in a bowl. Cover with water and soak for up to 8 hours. Drain and rinse well.

2. Put the soaked sesame seeds and figs, along with the banana, hemp seeds, cinnamon, nutmeg, cloves, turmeric if using, and the lemon juice in a blender. Add 1 cup / 225 ml water and blend on high speed until completely smooth. Adjust the spices to your taste, if desired. Enjoy.

3 tablespoons sesame seeds

2 dried figs

Pinch of fine sea salt

1 frozen banana

2 tablespoons hemp seeds

½ teaspoon ground cinnamon

Pinch of freshly grated nutmeg

Pinch of ground cloves

Pinch of ground turmeric, for
  color (optional)

A little squeeze of lemon juice

SESAME SEEDS It may surprise you to learn that sesame seeds are an excellent source of essential minerals. Calcium for the prevention of osteoporosis and migraines, magnesium for supporting the vascular system, zinc for bone health, selenium for antioxidant protection, and copper for reducing inflammation are just a handful of the incredibly important roles these minerals play for us. The biggest surprise of all? By weight, sesame seeds have a higher iron content than liver!

PECAN CRANBERRY PIE

SERVES 8 TO 10

If you've only ever had the white sugar–white flour version of pecan pie, this one will blow your woolen socks off. It's shocking how healthy whole foods can produce such a rich and tasty dessert! And even though it will look as if you spent hours fussing over it, this pie whips up in no time. My version includes cranberries, which add a festive taste, texture, and color to the well-loved classic pecan pie. The sweet, gooey filling is made with a combination of maple syrup and barley malt, with the added creaminess of nut butter. It's a surprising and delectable combination with the contrast of the tangy cranberries and crunchy pecans. This pie will fill your house with the amazing aromas of the holidays, whether you're baking it for a seasonal celebration or no particular reason at all.

CRUST

1½ cups / 150g rolled oats

¼ cup / 60ml coconut oil or ghee

¼ cup / 60ml pure maple syrup

¼ teaspoon fine sea salt

½ teaspoon freshly grated nutmeg

FILLING

½ cup / 120ml barley malt syrup

¼ cup / 60ml pure maple syrup

2 tablespoons tahini or nut butter

1 teaspoon vanilla extract, or 1 vanilla bean, split lengthwise, seeds scraped out and reserved

1 teaspoon ground cinnamon

1 tablespoon arrowroot powder

1½ cups / 210g whole raw pecans

1½ cups / 150g fresh or frozen cranberries (do not use dried cranberries)

1. Preheat the oven to 350°F / 180°C.

2. Make the crust: Put the oats in a food processor and blend on the highest setting to create a rough flour. Add the coconut oil, maple syrup, salt, and nutmeg and blend to combine. When the dough comes together, remove it from the food processor, gather it into a ball, and put it in the center of a 9-inch / 23cm pie pan. Using wet hands, press the dough out to the edges and eventually up the sides. Prick holes in the dough with a fork. Bake the crust for 10 to 15 minutes, until golden. Remove the crust from the oven and let it cool. Leave the oven on.

3. Make the filling: Put the barley malt, maple syrup, tahini, vanilla extract or seeds, cinnamon, and arrowroot in the food processor and blend until smooth. Add 1 cup / 140g of the nuts and pulse to chop (do not fully blend them, as you want a chunky filling). Fold in the cranberries.

4. Pour the filling into the cooled crust. Decorate with the remaining ½ cup / 70g whole nuts, and bake until bubbling and evenly browned, 20 to 30 minutes.

5. Let the pie cool completely, and serve.

ROOIBOS-POACHED PEARS WITH RAW CHOCOLATE OLIVE OIL SAUCE

SERVES 4

This is one sexy dessert. I know what you're thinking: *poached pears? Thanks, Grandma.* Trust me, this is a very hip way to end a meal. What's even better is how amazingly simple yet flavorful it is, with a game-changing chocolate sauce that will replace all other chocolate sauces forever! This major update of a classic dessert uses rooibos tea instead of a sugary syrup as the poaching liquid. The pears become rich and caramel-y, and as a bonus, you can drink the pear-infused tea with the dessert! The sauce is a mind-blowing combination of raw chocolate and olive oil, a rich and silky match made in heaven. You don't even need a stove to make this one—just whisk the ingredients together for an instant yet sophisticated sauce.

¼ cup /15g loose-leaf rooibos tea or 8 rooibos tea bags

3 tablespoons raw honey or pure maple syrup

4 firm, ripe pears (about 6 ounces / 175g; Bosc and Conference varieties are the best for poaching)

Raw chocolate olive oil sauce (recipe follows)

1. Bring 4 cups / 1 liter water to a boil in a medium saucepan. Add the tea, remove the pan from the heat, and let it steep for at least 15 minutes (the longer the better). Strain out the leaves or remove the tea bags. Sweeten the tea with the honey. Return the pan to the heat and bring to a simmer.

2. Peel the pears and slice them in half lengthwise (remove the hard core). Slide the pears into the sweetened tea and simmer until tender, 15 to 20 minutes.

3. Pour chocolate sauce onto the center of each plate. Carefully remove the pears from the tea, and put 2 halves on each pool of sauce. Drizzle more sauce into the hollow center of each half. Serve warm.

RAW CHOCOLATE OLIVE OIL SAUCE

MAKES ABOUT ¼ CUP / 60ML, ENOUGH FOR 4 PEARS

3 tablespoons cold-pressed olive oil

1½ tablespoons pure maple syrup

Pinch of fine sea salt

3 tablespoons raw cacao powder

Whisk the olive oil, maple syrup, and salt together in a small bowl. Sift in the cacao powder, and whisk well to remove any lumps.

SALT 'N' PEPPER CHOCOLATE CHIP COOKIES

MAKES 16 COOKIES (V) (gf)

I know it sounds crazy, but food speaks to me. Literally. I recently had a serious craving for chocolate chip cookies and set out to make some classic sweet-and-salty treats. As I was putting the baking sheet in the oven, the cookies looked up at me and said: "Stop! We would be really delicious with some black pepper, too." Huh? Are you serious? What a strange request, I thought. But assuming the cookies knew best, I ground some black pepper, sprinkled it on top, and baked them. The final result was shockingly delicious! The dark bittersweet chocolate contrasted against the salty dough with its spicy pepper kick was completely addictive and tasted like it was simply meant to be. I am so glad they spoke up.

1. Preheat the oven to 325°F / 170°C. Line a baking sheet with parchment paper.

2. Melt the coconut oil in a small saucepan over low-medium heat. Whisk in the barley malt, water, and vanilla. Remove from the heat.

3. Blend the oats in a food processor until you have a rough flour. Transfer it to a large bowl and add the coconut sugar, salt, pepper, baking soda, and baking powder. Stir to combine. Add the coconut oil mixture to the dry ingredients and fold to combine. Fold the chocolate into the batter.

4. Spoon out balls of dough onto the prepared baking sheet, leaving at least 2 inches / 5cm between them (they spread a lot!). Garnish each cookie with a few flakes of sea salt. Bake for 13 to 15 minutes, until golden brown. Remove from the oven, let sit on the baking sheet for 5 minutes, and then transfer to a cooling rack. Store the cookies in a tightly sealed container at room temperature for up to 5 days.

1/3 cup / 80ml coconut oil

1/3 cup / 80ml brown rice syrup

2 tablespoons water or milk of your choice (nut, seed, rice . . .)

1 teaspoon vanilla extract

2½ cups / 250g gluten-free rolled oats

½ cup / 60g coconut sugar

½ teaspoon fine sea salt

1 teaspoon coarsely ground black pepper

½ teaspoon baking soda

2 teaspoons baking powder

½ cup / 70g chopped organic dark chocolate (80% or higher)

Flaky sea salt

COCOA POWDER Cocoa powder is made from cacao beans that are roasted, ground into a paste, compressed, and grated into a fine powder. There are two types of cocoa powder: "natural unsweetened" and "Dutch-processed." Natural cocoa has a slightly bitter taste whereas Dutch-processed has been treated to remove this flavor (which to me isn't that noticeable). When cocoa powder is Dutch-processed, many of the beneficial flavonols are destroyed. For this reason, I always purchase only natural unsweetened cocoa powder. Cocoa powder is to be used in baked goods, not raw food recipes.

BLOOD ORANGE CHOCOLATE CAKE

SERVES 10 TO 12

A few years ago on the blog, I made a huge layer cake for my birthday. The readers went wild, so the next year I did it again. After that I became obsessed with baking completely over-the-top desserts. Nothing makes me giddier than slicing into a ridiculously towering cake—it's like I'm a kid again and all my wildest dessert fantasies are coming true.

This time I've made a blood orange chocolate cake. It's topped with an insane dark chocolate frosting that I'm confident will replace any chocolate frosting you have ever made. It is so rich and thick, just like frosting should be, but there are only five ingredients and they are all good for you. (You're welcome.) The cake itself is so moist and rich, you won't believe it's vegan. If you want to make just one layer, the frosting is delicious with both the blood orange flavor and chocolate cake, respectively. (If you cannot find blood oranges, use regular organic oranges instead.)

1. Preheat the oven to 350°F / 180°C. Lightly oil two 7-inch / 18cm springform cake pans.

2. Make the chocolate cake batter: In a large mixing bowl, sift together the flour, cocoa powder, baking powder, baking soda, and salt. In a separate bowl combine the maple syrup, milk, coconut oil, and vanilla; whisk to combine. Pour the wet ingredients into the dry ingredients and whisk to remove any lumps. Quickly whisk in the vinegar.

3. Make the blood orange cake batter: In a large mixing bowl, sift together the flour, baking powder, baking soda, and salt. In a separate bowl combine the maple syrup, orange juice, orange zest, coconut oil, and vanilla; whisk to combine. Pour the wet ingredients into the dry ingredients and whisk to remove any lumps. Quickly whisk in the vinegar.

4. Pour each bowl of batter into its own prepared cake pan. Bake the cakes until a toothpick inserted in the center comes out clean, approximately 50 minutes. Set the cakes on a wire rack and let them cool for about 20 minutes, then remove the springform sides. Let the cakes cool completely (you may even want to bake them the night before).

CHOCOLATE CAKE

2 cups / 240g whole spelt flour

½ cup / 50g unsweetened cocoa powder

2 teaspoons baking powder

1 teaspoon baking soda

½ teaspoon fine sea salt

1 cup / 240ml pure maple syrup

1¼ cups / 310ml milk of your choice (nut, seed, rice . . .)

6 tablespoons / 90ml coconut oil, melted, plus extra for the pan

2 teaspoons vanilla extract

1 teaspoon apple cider vinegar

(RECIPE CONTINUES)

BLOOD ORANGE CAKE

2½ cups / 280g whole spelt
   flour

2 teaspoons baking powder

1 teaspoon baking soda

½ teaspoon fine sea salt

1 cup / 240ml pure maple syrup

1¼ cups / 280ml freshly
   squeezed blood orange juice
   (about 5 oranges)

Grated zest of 2 organic blood
   oranges

6 tablespoons / 90ml coconut
   oil, melted, plus extra for
   the pan

2 teaspoons vanilla extract

1 teaspoon apple cider vinegar

Dark chocolate date frosting
   (recipe follows)

5. Use a long knife to carefully slice each cake in half horizontally, creating four thin layers total.

6. Put one of the blood orange cake layers on a platter. Spread the top with about a quarter of the frosting. Put a chocolate cake layer on top, and spread with frosting. Repeat with the remaining layers. Serve. (The cake keeps rather well at room temperature, covered, for 5 days.)

BAKING POWDER You can make baking powder at home (1 teaspoon baking powder = ½ teaspoon cream of tartar + ¼ teaspoon baking soda). If you're buying baking powder, make sure it contains non-GMO cornstarch and that it is aluminum-free. Commercial baking powder with aluminum is "double-acting," meaning that part of the rise takes place before baking, while the other part occurs once the food comes into contact with the heat of the oven. If you are not leaving your batter sitting around for a long period of time, this ingredient is unnecessary—and what's more, it has been linked to health issues, such as Alzheimer's disease. Aluminum-containing baking powder also imparts a bitter, metallic flavor to baked goods. Make the switch, and you will definitely notice a difference.

DARK CHOCOLATE DATE FROSTING

MAKES ENOUGH FOR A 4-LAYER CAKE

4 cups / 600g pitted dates

½ cup / 60g raw cacao powder

½ teaspoon fine sea salt

Grated zest of 2 organic oranges

1 cup / 250ml rice milk

1. If the dates are really dry, soak them in warm water for an hour or so, until softened. Then drain the dates.

2. Combine the dates, cacao powder, salt, and orange zest in a food processor, and pulse to break up the dates. Then slowly add the milk with the processor running until you have a thick, silky frosting that is easy to spread. If you have any leftovers, store them, covered, in the fridge for up to 2 weeks.

STOCKING THE PANTRY

THIS SECTION IS MEANT to inspire you to elbow out some of the typical things you'd find in a pantry—white flour, white sugar, frozen dinners, packaged snacks, and processed foods—to make room for whole-food ingredients that will act as building blocks for simple, nourishing home-cooked meals. If you have wholesome ingredients on hand all the time, you'll be less likely to order in, snack on processed junk food, and rely on packaged convenience meals. You will also save money, because even though it may seem less expensive to buy a frozen dinner, nothing can compete with the low cost of buying grains and beans in bulk.

Now, I do *not* expect you to run to your kitchen and toss out everything you own. On the contrary, use up what you have if you are so inclined, and when you need more of that item, go to the health food store or shop online and purchase something good to replace it with. Over time, your pantry will become a different place, one that is full of healthy ingredients that you can use to create anything. This may be a process that spans months, even years, but take your time and enjoy the course of change. Not only will you taste the difference, but your body will feel it, too.

LEGUMES

Collectively, beans and lentils are called *legumes*. The legume family also includes alfalfa, clover, peas, mesquite, carob, and peanuts. Beans and lentils are typically the main source of protein in a plant-based diet. They are low in fat, calories, sodium, and cholesterol, and they contain both soluble and insoluble fiber to support proper digestion. Beans and lentils are inexpensive, widely available, and have a long shelf life. Store beans in airtight glass containers away from light and heat.

BEANS

BLACK BEANS (also known as turtle beans and *frijoles negros*): Black beans have an earthy flavor and work well in salads, or as a puree or dip to fill sandwiches and tortillas, and to thicken soups.

BUTTER BEANS: Butter beans are a type of lima bean and live up to their name: they are incredibly creamy and buttery, making a great spread alternative to butter. They are also delicious in stir-fries.

CHICKPEAS (also known as garbanzos or ceci beans): One of the most popular and versatile beans, chickpeas are the key ingredient in hummus and falafels, but also make dynamite soups and stews. They hold their shape after cooking, making them ideal for use in salads.

FAVA BEANS: Dried fava beans are particularly hearty and go well in soups and stews. If you can find them fresh in the summer months, they make a delicious salad. When using dried favas, peel off the tough outer skin after soaking them; it is bitter and unappealing to eat.

KIDNEY BEANS: Available in a range of colors, the most familiar kidney bean is the deep-red variety that is popular in chili and stews. They also go very well in rice dishes and cold summer salads.

MUNG BEANS: Unlike most beans, mung beans do not need to be soaked before cooking, although it is beneficial if you have the time. They are very often sold sprouted in grocery stores as "bean sprouts."

NAVY BEANS: Small, creamy navy beans can be used in any recipe that calls for white beans. I love to use them in baking instead of eggs, and as a puree to thicken soups without cream.

LENTILS

Lentils do not require pre-soaking, but I encourage you to soak them for up to 8 hours to improve the digestive qualities, preserve nutrients, and reduce the cooking time. Store them as you would beans, in airtight containers away from light and heat.

BELUGA LENTILS: These tiny black lentils are glossy and resemble caviar when cooked. Beluga lentils hold up well after boiling, so try them in salads or soups. Their flavor is earthy and a good complement to smooth cheeses like chèvre.

DU PUY LENTILS: Because du Puy lentils maintain their shape and sturdy texture after cooking, they are ideal for making salads or adding to pasta dishes. A little on the expensive side, du Puy lentils are grown in only one region in France, in volcanic soil without fertilizer. If you cannot find these lentils, use regular French green lentils instead.

GREEN AND BROWN LENTILS: These lentils are larger than the red ones and tend to hold together slightly better after cooking. They are ideal for adding body and texture to soups and stews.

RED LENTILS: Red lentils are amazing in soups (in fact my favorite soup, on page 221!) because they cook quickly. They lose their structure when cooked, so they are best in liquid-y dishes.

SPLIT PEAS: Split peas can be found in both green and yellow varieties. Although they are whole when they grow, they split in the drying process when their skins are removed. They are common in soups but can also make a great dip when pureed with olive oil, garlic, lemon, and spices. Split peas are a good replacement for lentils in most recipes.

WHOLE GRAINS

Since whole grains have all the original elements intact, they still contain their delicate oils, which can spoil. It is best to keep them in tightly sealed canisters in a cool, dry place for up to a month. For longer shelf life, store whole grains in the refrigerator or freezer.

GLUTEN-CONTAINING

BARLEY: Barley comes in two forms, "pearled" and "whole hulled," the latter being the more nutritious. Amazingly thickening, it is delicious in soups and stews.

BUCKWHEAT: Although its name suggests otherwise, buckwheat is not part of the wheat family. In fact, it isn't even a grain, but the seed of a plant related to rhubarb. *Kasha* is toasted hulled buckwheat and is popular as a breakfast cereal. Buckwheat is high in protein and minerals. One of my favorite recipes using buckwheat is Apple-Cinnamon Buckwheat Crispies (page 160).

GLUTEN-FREE

MILLET: Aside from quinoa and amaranth, millet has the most complete protein of any grain. It is also the only alkalizing grain, meaning that it is rich in minerals and contributes to overall good health. The flavor of millet is nutty and delicious, enjoyed hot or cold. Wonderful for breakfast with fresh fruit and maple syrup, as well as in salads.

OATS: I always use whole rolled oats (not quick oats). Oats are naturally gluten-free but are often handled in plants that process wheat and other gluten-containing grains. To ensure that oats are safe for those who are gluten-intolerant, check that the oats are certified gluten-free. Rolled oats have a relatively long shelf life of 2 or 3 months.

QUINOA: Quinoa is the seed of an herb, and is therefore not a true grain. Quinoa is very versatile, and its light texture works well in place of other grains, especially less nutritious bulgur wheat and couscous. You can find quinoa in a wide range of colors, but the most common are white, red, and black. Quinoa cooks in 15 to 20 minutes, making it perfect for those in a rush, although like any other grain, it is best to soak it overnight before cooking.

RICE: There are numerous varieties of rice, but I will highlight my favorites, all of which are whole-grain.

    SHORT-GRAIN BROWN RICE: This type of rice is my personal favorite. It is very rich and nutty, with hints of sweet vanilla when cooked. It's delicious with a little ghee stirred in.

    LONG-GRAIN JASMINE OR BASMATI BROWN RICE: These two types are similar, and I use them interchangeably, but the jasmine rice has a more floral scent and flavor.

BLACK RICE: This type of rice has a glutinous texture, and is therefore best enjoyed in rice puddings, risotto, and dishes that do not require light, fluffy grains. It is rich in anthocyanins and other antioxidants.

SPELT: Spelt berries have a sweet taste that works well in salads and stews and makes for a delicious risotto. They also keep well after cooking, so you can always make more than you need and store leftovers in the fridge for future meals.

WILD RICE: Wild rice is not actually rice; rather, it is the seed of a wild aquatic grass indigenous to North America. It is relatively expensive but is a special addition to many dishes, adding an earthy nuttiness and unique texture.

FLOUR

It may surprise you to discover that flour actually expires. Like the whole grains that flour is milled from, it too contains all the parts of the grain, including the delicate fats that can become rancid. For this reason, it is extremely important to store whole-grain flour in tightly sealed canisters in a cool, dry place. Store in the fridge or freezer if you use it only occasionally. If your flour smells off or tastes bitter, chances are it is rancid and should be tossed.

GLUTEN-CONTAINING

SPELT: Although there are many types of gluten-containing flour, to keep my life simple (and yours!), the recipes in this book specify only whole-grain spelt flour. Many people who have wheat allergies find that they can tolerate spelt. If you cannot find spelt, you can replace it with whole-grain wheat flour.

ARROWROOT: I use arrowroot powder (sometimes sold as arrowroot "flour") to replace cornstarch in my recipes because it is far less processed and even has some health benefits. The taste of arrowroot is also more neutral, making it an ideal thickener for more subtly flavored sauces, ice creams, and desserts.

BUCKWHEAT: Though it's somewhat of an acquired taste, buckwheat flour is probably my favorite and most-used gluten-free flour because it has a very strong, assertive flavor. It is very popular in pancakes and crepes, but I also like to use it in pie crusts, muffins, and scones.

CHICKPEA: Often referred to and sold as gram flour, ceci flour, garbanzo bean flour, or besan, chickpea flour is made from ground chickpeas. Great in falafels and essential for making socca (page 62), the flour can be found in Middle Eastern grocery stores.

CORN: I use both corn flour and cornmeal in this book. Corn flour is completely powdery, while cornmeal is gritty. Both are naturally yellow in color, the flour being pale yellow and cornmeal being a rich gold. I use both to make corn bread, pancakes, and muffins.

OAT: You can find oat flour in many specialty shops, but the easiest way to make the flour is by grinding rolled oats in a food processor. Oat flour has more flavor than wheat and lends a great hearty texture without being too heavy.

SWEETENERS

Processed sugar saps minerals from the body during its digestion, causes massive blood sugar spikes and subsequent energy lows, and acidifies the blood. Natural sweeteners possess a whole range of flavors and textures, which makes experimenting with different ones so much fun. Although these options are a far better alternative to white sugar, it is still important to note that they are high in calories and some, such as honey, are very high on the glycemic index. Sweeten responsibly!

LIQUID SWEETENERS

BARLEY MALT: Barley malt is produced by sprouting (or malting) whole barley grains. The end result is a very sticky, thick, dark brown syrup that's about half as sweet as white sugar. The flavor is distinctively malty and has a mellow sweetness—perfect in gingerbread, spice cakes, and sauces. My favorite use for barley malt is in pie, which makes the filling uniquely gooey. Purchase barley malt that contains only barley and water.

BROWN RICE SYRUP: This sweetener is derived by culturing cooked rice with enzymes that break down the starches, then straining off the liquid and cooking it. The resulting rich, thick syrup is about half as sweet as white sugar, with a caramel-like flavor. Look for one that contains only brown rice and filtered water, and use in coffee or tea.

HONEY: Unlike most other sweeteners, honey actually tastes of where it was made and of the flowers the bees gathered the particular nectar from. Honey also varies in consistency, ranging from a syrupy liquid to creamy and thick, like a spread. In any recipe that calls for honey in this book, I am referring to clear, liquid honey. Always buy organic, unpasteurized, unfiltered honey in a glass jar. Store your honey in an airtight container in a cool, dark place. If it begins to develop crystals, simply warm the jar in a pot of water on the stove until it liquefies again. Honey is special in that it is the only food that never goes bad!

MAPLE SYRUP: As a native Canadian, pure maple syrup is one sweetener that is close to my heart. When purchasing pure maple syrup, look for the grade B version, as it has a richer flavor and higher mineral content than grade A. I use maple syrup to sweeten hot beverages and green smoothies and to replace sugar in baked goods (reduce other liquids in the recipe, typically water or milk, by 3.4 ounces / 100ml or between $1/3$ to $1/2$ cup / 75 to 112ml for each cup of sugar replaced).

NONLIQUID SWEETENERS

COCONUT PALM SUGAR: With a look, feel, and flavor similar to brown sugar, but with more complexity, it's the no-brainer replacement for white or brown sugar in any recipe because of its ideal 1:1 substitution ratio. Coconut palm sugar's low melt point and high burn temperature make it a perfect sweetener in baked goods and confections. Try it in sweet treats, or even in curries and sauces. Coconut palm sugar is low-glycemic, full of minerals, and sustainably harvested from the nectar of the coconut palm tree.

DATES: I couldn't live without dates because they are a whole food and a sweetener, retaining all of the original nutrients nature intended. My favorite type is the Medjool date because it is tender, rich, and sweet, with a complex, almost caramel-like flavor. Buy dates that are heavy for their size, plump, and moist. Look for organically grown dates, or give nonorganic ones a good wash before eating.

NUTS

It is best to buy nuts and seeds in the shell (their natural packaging) whenever possible; stored this way they will keep for up to 1 year. (Shelled nuts and seeds will keep for 3 to 6 months.) To ensure quality, visit a shop that you know has a high turnover (to ensure freshness), and taste the nuts before purchasing. Purchase organic whenever possible, as pesticides and toxins tend to accumulate in high-fat foods, such as nuts and seeds. Never buy "roasted" nuts and seeds (these are often deep fried!) or those processed with oil, salt, sugar, or other additives. Roasted nuts and seeds contain rancid fats and are a source of harmful free radicals. Nuts and seeds should always be purchased raw and unsalted, and then soaked or lightly toasted and seasoned at home if desired. For information on soaking nuts, see page 23. Store all nuts in the refrigerator in sealable glass containers.

ALMONDS: Almonds are great for making homemade nut milk and flour (commercially available as "almond meal"). If you have soaked some almonds, remove the skin and rinse the nuts well before consuming, as the peel contains enzyme inhibitors.

CASHEWS: Cashews blend up into the most amazing cream, which can be prepared either savory or sweet. This makes a wonderful dairy replacement in almost all uses.

HAZELNUTS: Naturally sweet and wonderfully versatile, hazelnuts are a great nut to have on hand to add a special touch to your meals. Look for hazelnuts in the shell, without cracks or holes. Hazelnuts are my favorite for making nut butter because they have such a rich, decadent flavor and creamy consistency due to their high oil content.

PECANS: Pecans are delicate, sweet, and mild, with a kind of softness that really complements leafy salads and desserts. Pecans are susceptible to spoilage after shelling, so keep them in the fridge or freezer to extend their shelf life.

WALNUTS: Walnuts make delicious raw "flour" for both baked and raw desserts. Walnuts are the only nuts that I do not soak, as their skins become too bitter and totally unpalatable.

SEEDS

Just like nuts, seeds should be purchased in a shop where you know they are fresh, especially if buying in bulk. Because of their smaller size, seeds will maintain freshness for 1 to 2 months after purchasing, and a little longer if stored in the fridge. Treat all seeds the same way you would treat nuts, storing them in glass away from heat and light.

FLAX SEEDS: Although it's true that flax seeds are high in omega-3 essential fatty acids, the main benefit of eating the whole seeds is their high fiber content. Ground flax seed contains many other nutrients and can be sprinkled on top of cereal and salads, added to soups at the end of cooking, or blended into smoothies. It is best to buy flax seeds that are whole and grind them yourself at home in a blender or coffee grinder, or with a mortar and pestle.

PUMPKIN SEEDS: Also known as *pepitas,* pumpkin seeds are one of my favorite seeds for punching up salads and sprinkling on stews. Lightly toasting them in a dry pan will puff the seeds up and bring out their amazing flavor.

SESAME SEEDS: Sesame seeds are available both hulled and unhulled. The unhulled seeds still have the bran intact and are a much better source of calcium, iron, and phosphorus than those without the bran. I always keep both brown (unhulled) and black sesame seeds on hand. Sesame makes a delicious, calcium-rich milk (see page 23).

SUNFLOWER SEEDS: Sunflower seeds are an inexpensive, versatile, and nutritious seed to add to baked goods, morning oats, salads, and dessert crusts. If you are buying shelled sunflower seeds from a bulk bin, smell them before purchasing to ensure they are indeed fresh.

FATS

The overwhelming majority of vegetable oils we find on grocery shelves today are highly refined. In fact, the clear, flavorless oils we've grown so accustomed to eating have distorted our palates away from rich-tasting, unrefined oils, even though they are far superior in flavor and health properties. Purchasing refined, low-quality oils and cooking with them sacrifices not only flavor but, most importantly, your health. Here are the basic rules for purchasing and storing oils.

1. Purchase only *unrefined cold-* or *expeller-pressed* plant-based oils; check for those words on the label of the bottle. This means that the oil was extracted on the first pressing, processed at lower temperatures without chemicals, and still contains the most nutrition and flavor.

2. When buying butter, always choose an organic brand from grass-fed cows, local if possible. If making ghee, purchase organic unsalted butter.

3. Always buy oils in the darkest bottle you can find (dark green, blue, or black). Never buy oil in a clear glass bottle, as light will destroy its nutrients and cause the oil to spoil more quickly.

4. Always buy oils stored in glass or ceramic (metal is okay if the bottle is BPA-free). Never buy oil stored in plastic because toxins in plastic can leach into the fat, and you will then ingest them.

5. Avoid fats that are solid at room temperature, such as lard, shortening, and margarine. Exceptions to this rule include ghee and coconut oil.

6. Never reuse oils that have been previously heated or, especially, used for frying. After heating, a fat is likely oxidized and therefore very harmful to your health!

7. Before opening, store oils in a cold, dark place. After opening, store oils in the fridge (flax oil can be kept in the freezer).

RAW OILS

I use these types of fats exclusively in their raw form to preserve their delicate nutrition. I use them to make salad dressings, dips, and sauces and add them to hot dishes as a garnish. It is possible to cook with some of these oils, but be aware of their lower smoke points (the temperature at which they will burn, indicated in parentheses).

OLIVE OIL: (320°F / 160°C) There are enough olive oil varieties to make your head spin. When purchasing olive oil, try to choose oils that are unrefined and cold-pressed, and avoid those with the word "pure" on the label. (This misleading term frequently means that the oil was extracted using solvents at high temperatures, with a minor percentage of virgin olive oil added back for flavor.) Tastes and aromas of olive oil vary greatly according to region and the actual olives used, so experiment with several varieties to find the one you like the best. Olive oil will keep for 2 to 3 months after opening, so buy only the amount you need and use it up. Store in the fridge.

Extra-virgin olive oil's low smoke point means that it is not suitable for stir-frying, sautéing, or any other high-heat cooking. Pour it all over your salads for sure, but stop using it to cook.

SESAME OIL: (350°F / 180°C) Purchase only cold-pressed sesame oil. Although most of us are familiar with "toasted" sesame oil, this type is often rancid and should be consumed in moderation (and used only as a garnish, not as a cooking oil). Cold-pressed sesame oil contains a natural antioxidant, sesamol, which helps prolong its shelf life. It is for this reason that ancient Indian teachings suggest that sesame is one of the most stable oils.

COOKING FATS

I use these two fats exclusively for cooking, including sautéing, oven roasting, and frying. Especially when cooking something in a pan on the stove, it is nearly impossible to know how hot the oil is and to regulate its temperature. To ensure that I am not burning my oil, I use a fat with a high smoke point, such as ghee or coconut oil.

COCONUT OIL: (400°F / 200°C) Refined, expeller-pressed, nonhydrogenated coconut oil is my favorite fat for cooking and baking. It is flavorless and odorless, so you won't end up with tropical-tasting food! Virgin coconut oil has additional health benefits, but it also lends a strong coconut flavor, which isn't always appropriate. Because expeller-pressed coconut oil is often manufactured at low temperatures, it is also suitable for use in raw foods, such as desserts.

GHEE/CLARIFIED BUTTER: (480°F / 250°C) One of the very few animal products in my current diet is ghee, also known as clarified butter. I choose to cook with ghee because of its very high smoke point, meaning it is safer to use when cooking at high temperatures. It is also a better choice than margarine and most refined oils because it is minimally processed. Ghee lends the most incredible aroma to foods, which you simply cannot achieve with plant-based fats. Because ghee is essentially concentrated butter, a little goes a long way!

VINEGAR

APPLE CIDER VINEGAR: If you were to keep just one type of vinegar in your refrigerator, this would be the one. Made from fermented apple cider, apple cider vinegar should always be purchased organic, unpasteurized (raw), unfiltered, and with the "mother"—the weblike strands floating around inside the bottle that indicate natural fermentation. It has a distinctly sharp tang that complements all types of food. Apple cider vinegar is wonderful for use in vinaigrettes, dressings, and sauces. It is rich in enzymes, aids digestion, alkalinizes the body, and supports a healthy immune system. A true miracle food!

BROWN RICE VINEGAR: Made by fermenting brown rice with koji (a culture), brown rice vinegar has about half the sharpness of apple cider vinegar, with a hint of sweetness. Use it for sushi rice, rice salads, or for dressing up steamed vegetables. Look for brown rice vinegar that has been brewed and aged naturally, with no ingredients other than cultured brown rice, koji, and water. High-quality brands will also contain the "mother."

SALT

In this book, I use both fine sea salt and flaky finishing sea salt. In any recipe that calls for a specific amount of salt (e.g., 1 teaspoon sea salt, such as in a baking recipe), I am referring to fine salt. For garnishing and seasoning to taste, I use a finishing salt because its coarse texture makes it easy to pinch between your fingers and sprinkle onto foods.

Sea salt is made by channeling ocean water into large clay trays and allowing the sun and wind to evaporate it naturally. Within this category there are a number of different grades, colors, and harvesting methods. In general, sea salt is my go-to seasoning because it is natural, flavorful, and contains vital trace minerals such as iodine, magnesium, and potassium that many of us are missing in our diets.

FINE GRAIN SALT: Fine salt is what I use in all of my recipes because it is easy to measure. It is available in both sea salt and Himalayan rock salt, and you can use either one for my recipes.

FLAKY SEA SALT: This is a fantastically flaky salt that is produced by carefully raking the crystals by hand, a technique that allows the crystals to remain intact. The large and beautiful crystalline texture makes it perfect as a finishing salt and for garnishing. Unlike most salts, flaky salt melts on your tongue and on hot foods while adding a great crunch. It is also less "salty" than other types of salt. Some types of finishing salt I use are Maldon, Murray River, and Cyprus Black Lava.

HIMALAYAN CRYSTAL/ROCK SALT: This is the pink salt that is now commercially available in many forms, including full rocks, chunks for salt grinders, coarse grain for cooking, and fine for baking. The array of elements and trace minerals in crystal salt are highly bioavailable, meaning that our bodies can easily absorb them. The flavor of Himalayan crystal salt is very pure and will greatly improve the taste of your favorite foods. It stores for a very long time without clumping, so look for it in the form that suits your needs.

SOYBEAN-BASED SEASONING

Most people assume that soybean-based seasoning is just for Asian food, but I actually add it to all kinds of soups, stews, dressings, and sauces. Instead of just being salty, soy seasoning adds amazing depth and umami flavor to foods. Traditionally, soybean-based seasoning is made with soybeans and sometimes wheat. The beans are first soaked, drained, and boiled. The cooked beans are cooled and inoculated with mold spores, and the entire mixture is cultivated for several days. The next step is mashing and combining the beans with a salt brine. This mixture is aged for several months, or sometimes years.

The final step is pressing the liquid out of the aged soybean mash—this liquid is the soy sauce; the residual mash is the miso.

I highly recommend purchasing good-quality soy products whenever possible. Choosing soy sauce and miso is like choosing a good bottle of olive oil or wine: look for the terms *traditionally brewed*, *organic*, and *non-GMO*. This is one condiment I would not compromise on. The conventional and less expensive versions of this seasoning may contain food dyes, refined sweeteners, preservatives, and chemical residues from processing. Always remember to keep soy sauces and miso in the refrigerator; opened soy condiments will keep for 2 to 3 months.

MISO: *Miso* is a Japanese word meaning "fermented beans." Traditionally, miso is made from soybeans and is found in the form of a thick paste. The process of making miso is similar to that for soy sauce; soaked and cooked beans are mashed and inoculated with koji (a specific mold spore) and salt. This mixture is left to ferment for months or years. The liquid that comes out of this process is tamari. Miso is available in many colors, depending on the legumes and grains used and the length of fermentation.

SHOYU: This is the Japanese word for "soy sauce." Shoyu is traditionally used as a condiment or seasoning after cooking and for dipping sushi. *Nama shoyu,* typically used in raw food recipes, is unpasteurized soy sauce. However, because the vast majority of soy sauces are heated to about 118°F / 48°C during pasteurization, you must read the label to confirm that the sauce is truly "raw." Many brands label themselves *nama shoyu* even though they have been pasteurized.

SOY SAUCE: This is a Chinese seasoning of which there are two varieties: light and dark. The light one is lighter in color with a low viscosity and is extremely salty. This type is more expensive than the dark and is used as a condiment at the table. Dark soy sauce is deep in color with a higher viscosity and a sweeter flavor (usually due to additives such as caramel color and/or molasses). Dark soy sauce is used more frequently in cooking.

TAMARI: If you are going to have any one of these sauces in your pantry, I would choose tamari. Tamari is another type of soy sauce, but perfect for people with gluten intolerance, as it is traditionally brewed without wheat (check the label to be 100% sure). Tamari has a stronger flavor than shoyu. It is usually used to season longer-cooking foods such as soups, stews, and baked dishes.

SUPERFOODS

The term *superfood* is a relatively new one. Although there is no set definition, the term refers to a class of exceptionally potent, nutrient-dense foods that act as both sustenance and medicine. Yes, they are typically expensive, but they are needed only in small quantities and each one has special properties for occasions when nothing else will do.

BEE POLLEN: My favorite superfood! I sprinkle this stuff on everything from morning oats to raw chocolate and everything in between. The flavor is slightly floral, and the taste varies among brands according to which flowers the bees were harvesting from. Most health food and natural food shops now carry bee pollen—it can sometimes be found right next to the honey—but the best quality bee pollen will be found in the fridge or freezer section. Bee pollen contains nearly every single nutrient the human body needs to survive. It is 20% to 35% protein by weight, including all twenty-two amino acids.

CACAO: Not to be confused with cocoa, cacao is raw, meaning that it retains all of its original nutrition, powerful antioxidants, and fragile enzymes. Cacao comes in several forms: whole beans, nibs (roughly chopped beans), and powdered (pulverized beans). Purchase organic and fair-trade whenever possible. Cacao is one of the most nutritionally dense foods on the planet, containing the highest concentration of antioxidants and magnesium of any food in the world!

CACAO POWDER: Purchase organic cacao powder whenever possible to avoid potential pesticide residues, which are heavily used in growing cacao beans. I use cacao powder to make raw chocolate and to add to smoothies and warm drinks. Super energy-producing! Store in the fridge or freezer to extend its shelf life.

CACAO NIBS/WHOLE BEANS: Nibs are the bits of crushed cacao bean. Like the powder, cacao nibs are extremely healthy, with an intense chocolate flavor, but aren't sweet at all. Cacao nibs should be crunchy, yet tender. Store in the fridge or freezer to extend their shelf life.

CHIA SEEDS: Chia seeds are so rich in antioxidants that they can be stored at room temperature for long periods without becoming rancid. Unlike flax seeds, chia seeds do not need to be ground to make their nutrients available to the body. You can purchase chia seeds at most health food stores.

CHLORELLA: Much like spirulina, chlorella is a single-celled, water-grown algae. Purchase organically grown, dark-green chlorella in powder form. Mix it into smoothies to hide the rather unpleasant taste. One tablespoon of chlorella provides 320% of the RDA of iron and 120% of calcium.

GOJI BERRIES: When buying goji berries, purchase organic whenever possible, to avoid those fruits sprayed with chemical pesticides and/or sulfur dioxide. The berries should feel like raisins: slightly moist but not mushy (and not too dry). The color should be deep red. Goji berries are very high in antioxidants and are very good sprinkled on yogurt, blended into smoothies, and added to muesli or baked granola.

HEMP SEEDS: Also known as "hemp hearts," these are available in several forms; the hulled seed is my favorite. Hemp seeds make a wonderful milk (see page 23). I also toss a few tablespoons into my smoothies to make them creamy, sprinkle them on my morning cereal, and add them to salads. Their flavor is rather mild, but the seeds boost the protein and omega fats in whatever you add them to.

LUCUMA: Lucuma is a fruit native to Peru. It is dried and pulverized and sold as a powder, which can be used for sweetening smoothies, ice cream, cakes, pies, and yogurt. I love making a raw caramel from lucuma and dates, or simply mixing lucuma with a nut butter to spread on raw crackers. It is a fantastic sugar and flour substitute, without the empty calories.

MACA: Maca is the highest-altitude crop on Earth, cultivated in the Andean mountains of Peru. Although it resembles a large radish, maca is a member of the Brassica family of plants (broccoli, cabbage, kale, etc.). Look for maca sold as the dried, powdered root for easiest consumption. As it is naturally high in minerals, you can add maca to smoothies and raw chocolate for a nutrient boost.

SPIRULINA: Spirulina is a single-celled, blue-green spiral algae that grows naturally in lakes and waterways all over the Earth and is now also grown for commercial purposes. To purchase, look for a richly pigmented dry powder, preferably organic, that smells fresh. Mix it into smoothies, raw puddings, or ice cream. Spirulina contains astounding levels of chlorophyll, protein, vitamins, major and trace minerals, essential fatty acids, and antioxidants.

WATER

Water varies greatly depending on where you live. In North America, most municipal water is chlorinated, which is meant to kill disease-causing bacteria that the water or the transport pipes may contain.

In all of the recipes in this book that require fermentation (soda, yogurt, cheese, etc.), it is essential that you use nonchlorinated water, as chlorine will also kill lactobacillus, the friendly bacteria that we want to propagate! If the bacteria die, the recipes will not work.

You can easily buy nonchlorinated water at any grocery store (distilled, reverse osmosis, or spring water will work). Alternatively, you can boil water and let it cool, or let water sit in a jar or bowl, uncovered, for 24 hours, allowing most of the chlorine to evaporate.

WITH BOUNDLESS GRATITUDE

It takes a village to write a cookbook, this much I know is true. This project would not have been possible without the help and support of so many friends, family, and talented experts to whom I am eternally grateful.

First, to my husband, Mikkel, thank you for always believing in me, even when I doubted myself. Thank you for your unwavering love and support when I was wavering. Thank you for late-night market trips, rubbing my aching shoulders, taste-testing every single recipe, and making me laugh through it all. I love you more than tahini. Almost.

To my son, Finn, thank you for being with me every step of this adventure. Your spirit is woven into every one of these pages, and I look forward to the day you will understand that. I can't wait to play in the kitchen together.

To my parents: Dad, thank you for ceaselessly encouraging me to follow my dreams. This cookbook proves that you are right: nothing is impossible. Thank you also for being my moral compass, my ray of positive light, and for reminding me that life is supposed to be fun. Mum, thank you for honoring my obsession with composition, color, and light. Thank you for listening to me wail about misplaced broccolini and for totally understanding why that napkin does not go with that plate. Thank you for countless hours of schlepping, prepping, cleaning up, prop hunting, and blueberry foraging. Working on this together has been a highlight of my life, and I feel so lucky to have shared this journey with you. This may be a cookbook to many, but to us it is a volume of precious memories. I hope you're ready for round two!

To Brooke, thank you for filling my home with your love and light. Thank you for finding solutions and staying positive when cakes collapsed and sauces took a trip to wrongtown. Thank you for ignoring weirdos in the bushes to get the perfect shot! Thank you for inspiring me to always trust my heart and hands in the kitchen. I'm first in line to buy your cookbook, someday.

To Samantha, for being such an amazing manager, but above all, for being my dear friend. You have gone beyond the call of duty more times than I can count, and please know how deeply grateful I am for everything you do. You have taught me how far I can go with a little push and how much bigger I can dream with another head on the pillow. Drop the mic.

To my incredible team of recipe testers, I owe you one. Gina Johnston, Debbie Levy, Trevor Britton, Alexandra Wylie, Anastasia Doudakis, Jaime Tan, Valerie Orviss, Natasha Tay, Jennifer Northrup, Brigitte Hendrix, Kaitlin Kazmierowski, Demelza Rafferty-Pou, Kristine Lye, Julie Leach, Alicia Key, Anna Gavan, Mia Hunt, Jane Matthews, Neeza Adenan, Virginia Coatsworth, Stephanie Kafoury, Meredith Rosenbluth, Sheila Britton, Natasha Figueroa, Stephanie Bonic, Gertrud Sol Lund, Renee Barker, Elizabeth Ball, Vanessa Bradshaw, Karen Watson, Willemien Van Egmond, Paula Hannon, Anne Lockie, Dani Dunlevy, Michele Dellios, Eline Stampe, Kelly McVerner, Therese Eriksson, Ambar Surastri, and David Koch. Thank you for your love and support of what I do and for being so eager to carefully re-create my meals in your kitchens. Your time, energy, and thoughtful feedback were more helpful than I can express, and I hope that I have made you proud.

To Rune, thank you for making my images come to life. You are a genius.

To Rica Allannic, my editor at Clarkson Potter, your enthusiasm for what I do has meant so much to me. Thank you for believing in this project and supporting my vision so graciously every step of the way.

To Robert McCullough, my editor at Appetite, I knew from our very first conversation that working together was going to be serious fun. Thank you for bringing so much light and joy into the process, and for championing me every step of the way.

To Marysarah Quinn, my book designer, thank you for being so darn patient with me and allowing this to be a collaborative effort. Together, we have made something truly beautiful.

To the rest of the team at Clarkson Potter, Aaron Wehner, Doris Cooper, Jessica Freeman-Slade, Terry Deal, Heather Williamson, Erica Gelbard, and Carly Gorga, thank you for all of your hard work and expertise.

To Sharon Bowers, my literary agent, thank you for always being there to answer my zany questions, quell my insecurities, and help me believe that I could, in fact, pull this off. Your experience, expertise, and humor have meant the world.

Last, to my readers. My heart bursts with gratitude for each and every one of you who has ever made a recipe from the blog. Thank you for trusting me that bread can change your life, that raw brownies are better than cooked ones, and that cheesecakes can be made out of nuts. Thank you for following *My New Roots* with so much delight, allowing me into your kitchens, and spreading the healthy word right alongside me. Together we are building a community of healthy, conscious people who will not take white flour for an answer.

INDEX